Understanding Marriage

SWAMI PARAMANANDA

Order this book online at www.trafford.com/07-1234
or email orders@trafford.com

Most Trafford titles are also available at major online book retailers.

Note for Librarians: A cataloguing record for this book is available from Library and Archives Canada at www.collectionscanada.ca/amicus/index-e.html

ISBN: 978-1-4251-3286-6

We at Trafford believe that it is the responsibility of us all, as both individuals and corporations, to make choices that are environmentally and socially sound. You, in turn, are supporting this responsible conduct each time you purchase a Trafford book, or make use of our publishing services. To find out how you are helping, please visit www.trafford.com/responsiblepublishing.html

Our mission is to efficiently provide the world's finest, most comprehensive book publishing service, enabling every author to experience success. To find out how to publish your book, your way, and have it available worldwide, visit us online at www.trafford.com/10510

www.trafford.com

North America & international
toll-free: 1 888 232 4444 (USA & Canada)
phone: 250 383 6864 • fax: 250 383 6804 • email: info@trafford.com

The United Kingdom & Europe
phone: +44 (0)1865 722 113 • local rate: 0845 230 9601
facsimile: +44 (0)1865 722 868 • email: info.uk@trafford.com

10 9 8 7 6 5 4 3

CONTENTS

Foreword

The understanding and interpretation of the institution of marriage must necessarily rest on its spiritual foundation and assume its sacred significance. It is in this context that Swami Paramananda's book needs to be welcomed in our midst where confusion reigns supreme with regard to marriage. This sacred union has been used since time immemorial as an ideal cradle for the procreation of the species and has offered institutional structures for the psychological meeting of male and female energies for mutual advancement and enhancement.

There are as many views on marriage today as there are individuals and the flexibility of its form and purpose has gone through several mutations and permutations lending credence to the view that it is an institution which is neither permanent nor inflexible. Swamiji's book aerates the varied arguments around this issue and explores the pros and cons of the age-old union of the sexes both in traditional and modern terms. His spiritual yet practical standpoint allows the reader to understand its unusual implications and mystical undertones.

How can we in the light of this understanding explore this institution and its relevance for modern times? What is the role of the man and the woman to make marriage a viable union to further the nurture of children and the welfare and happiness of mankind? What is the meaning of spiritual growth in marriage for the couple? What does each partner bring to fruition in the evolution of this institution? Are the rules governing marriage inviolable or can they be modified to suit the times and the temperaments of the partners?

What is indeed the goal of marriage and in what way does it pave the way for peace and love in the home, community and the world? In the pages that follow, many of you will find the answer to your myriad questions. I wish you a happy journey to yourself and to the other through whom you can find yourself!

Shakuntala Hawoldar

Preface

'Understanding Marriage' is the seventeenth book of Swami Paramananda written with the objective of sensitizing people on lost or corrupted values, which were once basically aimed at assisting people to realize the ultimate purpose of human life: enlightenment.

Marriage found its origin in the primitive society through physical attraction of the opposite sexes and with human evolution it assumed a sacred place in human life. Thus, various kinds of religious marriages emerged, with very lofty rituals. However, with time, they lost their true worth to become social conventions or traditions.

In this book, Swami Paramananda explains the basic differences between man and woman, while at the same time emphasizing that we have both masculine and feminine characteristics within us, the predominance of one defining our specific gender. However, the ultimate union or marriage is that of the inner man and woman, for which the help of the outer man or woman is essential to a certain extent.

The degeneration of marriage, which is the basis of family life, has led to various social ills we are facing today. The rising rate of divorce, adultery, jealousy, possessiveness and broken families are but a few of them. For the situation to change, it is of paramount importance that people have a clear understanding of marriage and the responsibilities it incurs.

This book of Swami Paramananda is indeed a rare, but bold attempt to expose truths that are tactically avoided, supposedly not to hurt people's sensibilities, regardless of the great harm this is causing to society.

A. M.

Introduction

Why Marriage?

The definition of the word marriage according to the dictionary is 'the lawful union of a man and a woman, by which they become husband and wife.' It is worth noting that no mention has been made of religion, caste, creed or sect, though in general people give much consideration to these factors. Also, two key words strike me in the definition, one is lawful and the other is union.

Some communities perform their wedding ceremonies in a church in the presence of a priest and God, for a church is supposed to represent God. Why bring God in a marriage? Is it a sacred or trustful act? If it is, then why bring the law in it? Why do we also contract a civil marriage? Union means a state of harmony or agreement. How can there be harmony when there is doubt? It must be doubt that brings in the law, is it not? We talk of union and harmony, we bring in God and religion, then very often we part and that too, not on good terms but at daggers drawn. Why all this? Why do we marry after all? Is it merely to imitate what others have always been doing? Is it for sex and children? But then, these do not require any ceremony, church, god, law and the hullabaloo of today's marriage!

Can we say that we marry to have company in old age? Well, this does not always work. Then for what do people marry? Do we have at least the courage to say boldly that we do not know and that we are victims of ignorance? If so many people since the dawn of humanity have been marrying and since the scriptures, which are the words of God, have mentioned it, then there must be something great about it. But what is it? Surely, the way it is done today does not reflect the truth that it may conceal.

Apart from the force of instinct and evolution for the propagation and sustenance of the species, which draws the opposite sexes together, there are social reasons that lead to marriage. Society is governed by a set of norms that its citizens have to follow, otherwise one becomes an odd man out. Getting married is one such norm. There is pressure from both society and parents to follow the trend. In fact, most parents consider it a burden if their children do not enter marriage, especially if they are girls. It should have been a prime concern for parents to fully educate their children about marriage and sex and let them choose. But this is far from being the case. People who are not revolutionaries are forced to follow the rules. Another reason why young people get into married life is that, being influenced by movies, novels and friends, they are induced into a dream world of fantasy, without realising the illusory nature of all these. The real problem, however, is that the whole of humanity is shrouded in ignorance related to marriage and sex.

What is the secret behind marriage? This is precisely what this book aims at, revealing the truth behind one of the most sublime stages of life. Subjects like marriage form part of what I call self-education. I invite the reader to join me on a journey into the real purpose of marriage.

The Origin of Marriage

I do not think any historian or scientist can trace out the exact time when marriage as a social convention began. One thing is sure, the opposite sexes have always been attracted to each other and this can be traced out because it started with the first animal creatures. Opposites attract and when there is attraction, there is a meeting on the physical and subtle levels. Very long ago, man and woman stayed together without going through any ritual or ceremony that could be called marriage. In the beginning it was a natural attraction. Later, with the advent of tribalism, a set of rites and rituals was invented, probably based on certain beliefs.

Some writers associate marriage to the biblical advent of Adam and Eve. According to the Bible, the first couple was Adam and Eve when God brought them together. But there is a big question. The original couple was thrown outside the Garden of Eden after they disobeyed the Lord by eating the forbidden fruit. It was then that they copulated and formed a family with Cain and Abel. The question is this: what if they did not eat the fruit? Would they still be in the garden? Would Eve have conceived? After they were cast out of the garden, did they perform any sort of ritual marriage or did they instinctively come together, which resulted in the birth of Cain and Abel?

If we reflect deeply, we will realise that the very basis of marriage is sexuality. It is an irresistible attraction between the opposite sexes. When animals come together, they do not reflect or think about having a family or living like a couple. They are simply attracted towards each other, but in the animal kingdom a price has to be paid. The male and the female are often put to test and most of the time it is the male which has to go through the physical capacity test. There is often a fierce competition between the males. In some species it is a test of quality. The female will copulate with the male with the best quality of sperm and it is a miracle how animals come to know about this through instinct.

In short, in the animal kingdom, it is a matter of survival of the fittest, a question of breeding to keep on with the propagation of one's species. All this is an awe-inspiring play of Mother Nature. In some species, the most aggressive male will be the leader of the harem, the reproductive element for the continuation of progeny. Some animals choose their mate by the sense of smell as the females release certain chemicals to signal their readiness for copulation or to purposely attract the male. In a few rare species, the animals are loyal to their partner and offspring, while in general most are polygamous.

We can see that many of the reproductive and sexual behaviours of animals have been inherited by man too. After all, we descend from them. Do we not reproduce? Do we not have a polygamous tendency? Here I am referring more specifically to male human beings, though there are exceptions. We can therefore conclude that attraction based on sex has been the predominant factor in the coming together of male and female, be it in the animal kingdom or the human world. Through sexual union come both family life and preservation of the species. Man, however, has a somewhat different story simply because he is man and not animal. We can say that he is a social animal, yet he is different from animals. His possibilities are tremendous, though his behaviour is weird. He is neither completely animal nor completely man. In fact, he has an identity crisis, which is why he is in a great conflict with others and himself.

Marriage or union is of divine origin. Only the mystics know that there is an eternal union of consciousness and energy, which are the substratum, womb and cause of not only one but innumerable universes. The Hindu scriptures have termed it as Purusha-Prakriti, that is, Consciousness-Energy. They are the Mother and Father of everything. Out of this union, all other dualities and multiplicities of existence are born. Satti-Shiva and Ardhanareshwar are amongst the other names given to that state. Light-darkness, matter-energy, fire-water, in short, all dualities of life and their interplay make possible this mysterious universe. In a poetic or devotional term, it can be said that the eternal couple Consciousness-Energy are the parents while everything else is their offspring. What Chinese have called yin-yang is nothing but the dual principle of life, manifesting in innumerable aspects in the form of the pairs of opposites.

Life is made up of opposite but complementary forces. In each pair of opposites, one duality complements the other. If there is only cold, life will not flourish and also if there is only heat, life will vanish. The very basis of life is dualistic matter and everyone is both male and female. At the surface all dualities are different, while at the base they merge. They do not possess each other, but become one.

Man and woman are each a universe in themselves. However, individually they do not normally manifest all the qualities of the universe, while united they have a greater possibility to form a complete universe. This is no wonder as each has different traits. This is why man is said to be incomplete and so is woman. They have to unite to make a whole. But alas! They are ignorant about the true aim of their own existence and in addition to that, they are conditioned and in conflict with themselves. When man is at odds with woman, he is in fact at odds with himself, and vice versa. The great conflict, frustration, sorrow and illusion that have engulfed humanity are caused by the ignorance and conditionings of both man and woman about themselves. Nature is working smoothly due to a perfect union and interplay of the dual forces, but what has happened to us human beings? It seems that a great mishap has befallen us since a very long time, yet we do not seem to know its cause or origin.

The purpose of married life is to help each other become a real image of God. Man is a potential Shiva, and woman is a potential Satti, but right now they are conditioned human beings.

They both have to break their conditionings in order to attain their divine nature. Hence we see that marriage has a divine origin and purpose.

Choosing a Partner

How do we choose our partner? A few choose a partner purely out of emotional attraction, while most people's choice is a calculated one. The reasons behind their choice range from physical beauty to the subsequent possession of much wealth. For one it is the hair, for another it is the face, still for another it is the shape of the body. Many young men contract loans to build a house and therefore seek to marry a girl who holds a job so as to be relieved from the burden. Some young people still choose their partner according to their caste and manage to create an emotion, which they call love. Such attitudes are very disgusting, especially at the dawn of the third millennium. Others look for status or degree of popularity. Many young people are mad after celebrities, without realizing that a person may be good in a field and yet have a demoniacal character. In fact, many celebrities have a disastrous and unstable married life. How great an illusion such people breed!

Do not think that those who are emotionally attracted are better off than those who make a calculated choice. What people call *coup de foudre* or love at first sight rarely ends up in a stable married life. There are definitely a few stable and lovely couples; nevertheless they are not successful partners because they do not know the real purpose of marriage. Yes, they may be leading a peaceful life without much trouble, but this does not imply that they have achieved anything spiritually. Apart from all these, we have the arranged marriage, which is normally discussed and settled mainly by parents or relatives. Nowadays, there is also the Internet or e-marriage where partners are chosen via the electronic mail. We even have matrimonial agencies offering their service against payment of a fee to arrange marriages, especially between foreign partners.

Yet another recent and popular means through which people get into contact and finally get engaged is the mobile phone. A few messages sent to an unknown person via SMS and it is done. Though many have had unpleasant surprises, people keep on trying with the hope that one day, they will come across the ideal partner of their dream. Of course, such trials have been flops. Some youngsters, having been emotionally caught, end up in early marriages. Others prefer to go out with a few partners, then later choose one with whom they can set sail for a permanent voyage into family life, but this hardly ever works.

If most marriages fail, is it because we choose the wrong partner or are there other causes? The first part of the question can be answered in affirmative, but it is not the only reason. Now, how to choose the right partner? This cannot be answered unless we know what the real purpose of married life is. Prior to that, it is of paramount importance to have an insight into the nature of human psyche and the purpose of human existence.

Man and woman are images of God, yet both are incomplete by themselves until they fully realize and express this truth. This is why it has been said that man or woman is only a half. However, being a half does not mean that one cannot live alone. There have always been a few who have remained celibates. In fact, there will always be some who will choose to live alone. Nevertheless, they are exceptions and that too in a given incarnation, as they must have experienced life with the opposite sex in a previous birth. Otherwise their evolution would be incomplete. After all, the universe is both male and female, yin and yang. Neither the sperm nor the ovum is complete in itself.

Experiencing the fact that each human being is an image of God is the ultimate possibility of our existence because God is the ultimate truth. Such a realization gives man and woman the status of a god. God is infinite bliss, freedom, eternal peace and infinite power, while a god is a reflection of these attributes. Man can live his life as he chooses, but existence moves in such a direction as to lead man towards that realization. In fact, the universe was created for that purpose. Not endeavouring to attain it would be illogical and unscientific. Man's body is conceived in a way that is conducive to that end. The endeavour leading to the ultimate experience should be a matter of intelligence, adventurous spirit, understanding and love. However, since millennia, the lofty aims of life as well as the sacred knowledge have been distorted. Consequently we live like brutes.

Married life can help us greatly in achieving our ultimate possibility. A person who wishes to embark on the spiritual adventure should be wise in choosing the right partner and in this matter the advice of an enlightened being is of paramount importance. I have given a glimpse of the ultimate purpose of human existence; now let us briefly look at the psychic aspect of human beings. In fact, I have dealt with this subject extensively in my previous works.

Man and woman are both very complex beings. Their bodies are made such that they can come into contact with each other, not only for the purpose of procreation but essentially for experiencing life to its deepest core. Sex, for instance, is not only for procreation but also for realizing that there is a point where there is a complete dissolution of one's being for a fraction of a second, which brings bliss. It is indeed a very intimate and deep union. However, it is so quick and fleeting that before we have the time to realize what transpired, it is all over.

Let us go deeper into the psyche of man and woman. Both have seven bodies. The first four have gender, while the fifth, sixth and seventh are genderless as they are not bodies in the literal sense. In most people, the first four layers are not fully developed and seldom do they evolve beyond the first and second bodies, that is, the physical and emotional ones. Few people reach the third and still very few, the fourth body. The fifth is the spiritual layer, which is difficult to reach and is a rare phenomenon. The sixth one is the cosmic body. Yogis, enlightened beings and avatars have realized it and have even gone beyond to attain the seventh sky or Nirvana.

The first body of a woman is female while her second one is male, the third or the astral body is again female while her mental body is male. For man, it is the opposite. His physical and astral bodies are male, while his emotional and mental bodies are female. When his emotional body is fully developed, a man will become very receptive, emotional and sympathetic. In brief, he will manifest the traits of a woman according to the degree of development of the second body. Normally, the man retains his masculinity, but it may also happen occasionally that a man is dominated by his emotional body and thus feminine qualities become predominant. This may happen for various reasons, which could be psychological, circumstantial (that is, by the force of circumstances) or karmic (that is, based on reactions from past incarnations).

Of course, these can be explained scientifically because such a person will manifest physical signs. For example, there may be an abnormal amount of certain hormones in his body. It may be discovered that he has less testosterone or his Y chromosome may be associated with a small x, which symbolically will appear as Yx. Such a man may have manly qualities but with a dominance of female traits. He can have an erection and impregnate a woman, yet will lack the character of a normal man. For instance, he may be less aggressive and adventurous. If such a person marries a woman whose emotional body too is developed, then male traits will tend to dominate in her behaviour because a woman's emotional body is male by nature. Many conflicts in a conjugal life result from such situations. Nevertheless, if the woman retains her essential feminine traits and the man too retains most of his masculine traits during the development of their respective emotional bodies and if both are aware of the subtle changes operating in them, then no major problem will arise.

Conflicting situations may also arise when the other subtle bodies develop. If the development is sane and the persons are meditating, then problems may be avoided, otherwise life becomes a nightmare. Imagine a situation where a woman has reached her emotional body and the man is hovering around his first body, which is male, or is at the astral body, which is also male. It will be like two male characters living together as husband and wife. When referring to this type of situation, people will say, "Two men cannot live together!" For the purpose of evolution, friction between the positive and negative is important. Similarly, many women would like their husbands to be real males or even macho, otherwise they are not a match for them.

Thus we find that there are vast basic differences between man and woman, and they are a must for the mental, emotional and spiritual evolution of both partners. However, these differences should be natural, not artificial. Today most people are artificial beings, thus the conflict between man and woman. Though different, each individual can have a partner who will help him or her to evolve spiritually. This leads us to what people have termed soul-mates, also known as *âmes soeurs*. In reality, there is no such thing because souls are neutral.

Man lives as a soul from his fifth or spiritual body and that is a state of pure light. It is therefore genderless, not to mention the sixth body, which is a higher state of the soul called *Brahma sharir* or cosmic body, which is a mass of pure energy. Then how has the term 'soul-mate' emerged? Nevertheless, it is true that everybody has at least one individual with whom one can be compatible. This has nothing to do with the soul but with the first four layers of our being, which are also related to zodiacal signs and our karma.

Soul-mates and the Zodiacal Signs

Souls being neutral, homogenous and one, the question of having another soul as partner does not arise. People, however, have different characteristics and two persons of opposite sex who can tread the path of spirituality in the normal course of life due to their being compatible can be called soul-mates. And according to me, each individual can be compatible with only one partner. This is the real reason why adultery becomes a relevant issue.

Bearing in mind that the first and ultimate purpose of human life is to realize and express our divine nature, it should be very clear that God has created human beings so as to live as couples for both material and spiritual evolution. In this endeavour, a partner of the opposite sex can be of much help, provided the right one is chosen. A wrong choice can cause much trouble and waste of precious time that needs to be dedicated to spiritual practice.

The characteristics of a soul-mate depend on the karma of the latter. I mean that the person must have reached a stage where it is possible to embrace spiritual life and where he or she is ready to tread the path in the company of the opposite sex with the view to progress spiritually. The problem is how to recognize such a person. For highly evolved souls, it is easy. Others will have to depend on certain factors like matching the horoscope, birth charts and auras. Most important of all is the horoscope.

Today people say that when you are in love, all these things are trivia, but I would like to see those who are really in love! Who can say that they will not end up in a divorce, a conflicting conjugal life or even murdering their partner? In fact, love is absent. Instead, there is an immature feeling, lust, desire and bargaining in the name of love. If those people, who pretend to have done a love marriage, had a real love affair, then their progeny would be either geniuses or gods and the world would be a paradise.

What is the horoscope? It is based on the specific characteristics possessed by each shape, defined by a zodiacal sign, formed by celestial bodies. A zodiacal sign becomes a structure whose vibration creates a harmony of sound or musical tone. The horoscope is derived from the science of astrology, which helps to determine the characteristics, inclinations, strengths and weaknesses of a person according to the date and precise moment of his birth. The horoscope can be used to predict his future and offer valuable information on various aspects of his life such as favourable and unfavourable moments, colours, zodiacal signs and many others.

Each celestial body has specific features. For example, the sun is a symbol of fire and fire has certain characteristics. It does not only burn but also purifies. Apart from symbolising the gross element of fire, it is also a sign of life and of brightness. The morning sun, for example, bestows many virtues and is good and important for our health. But the midday sun may cause skin cancer and other problems if we are exposed to it for too long. These are some of its gross tangible effects, but it also has subtle effects that few people know.

Inside tree trunks are circular patterns that register events like sun phases. These ring patterns have been found to become larger during sun flare cycles. Russian Professor Chijevsky discovered that each sun cycle, which occurs every eleven years, has direct effects on earth such as favouring the occurrence of wars, revolutions and so on. Another scientist found that it caused man's blood to become thinner while it is normally thicker than that of a woman. There are still subtler effects that celestial bodies have on human beings.

There are countless moving bodies, isolated or grouped, in space that are as if performing a dance to the tune of a music. All move according to the law of gravity. Every physical celestial body is a mass of stardust arranged in a very mysterious way. Each individual is directly related to one or more moving bodies.

Since each of them has different characteristics, each person's character will be unique. There are innumerable variations in the way the DNA of each person has been arranged, giving rise to specific characteristics. These must be in harmony with the characteristics of the celestial bodies, especially with the zodiac, otherwise the human 'system' can suffer from an imbalance.

Planets, stars and other moving objects are made of a few or all of the five main elements. Some are even a mixture of other elements. These make for the characteristics of the individual or group of celestial bodies. People who are born under them are directly influenced by their characteristics. Therefore a person who is born when Virgo is in ascendance will be under its influence. Ancient mystics have observed and studied the properties of the moving bodies in relation to events occurring on earth and the behaviour of people. This is how the science of astrology came to existence. Through this science, the general characteristics of a person can be known.

In the past, priests, who were advanced in the science, would prepare a birth chart of persons who wished to marry and see if they matched. Some people consult their horoscopes to know under which zodiacal sign their matching partner should be. Thus, when they come across potential partners, they simply need to check their date of birth in order to confirm whether they form a matching pair. Names too were given according to the characteristics of the sign of zodiac prevailing at the precise moment of birth of the individual. Today many people name their children according to their wish, without knowing that a name is a sound vibration that must match the music of the zodiacal sign.

Out of ignorance, we mock people when they talk about making birth charts to check whether the signs of two potential partners match. This attitude is most incorrect as celestial bodies do influence our characters. Hence, one way of choosing the right partner is to consider the latter's sign of zodiac and do the matching. However, man can, if he is determined, transcend the magical circle represented by the zodiac, but this demands tremendous energy and wisdom. Meditators and enlightened beings, who are very few, are able to go through such a super natural feat.

Therefore it is important to consider the astrological factor when choosing a partner. Let it be clear, especially to the rational mind, that it is not a question of superstition but a very subtle scientific reality. If it were a question of only physical matching, then astrology would not be of great importance. But we are much more than a mass of flesh, bones and marrow - we are a mind and a heart too. We are quite complex a being, nay, we are a whole universe! And above all, we are an image of God.

Finally, let it be understood that a man or a woman, who so desires, can tread the path alone and many have done it. If it has to be with a partner, then both must be very intelligent, honest and spiritual. Unfortunately, such persons are rare, though potentially we can all be very good partners. To actualize such a potential requires tremendous energy, patience, intelligence and sacrifice.

Love and Marriage

In the name of love, many ugly things have been done and are still being done. People have killed, raped, married, divorced, had children, oppressed, tortured, discriminated and what not! Here I would like to say a few words in regard to rape and lovemaking. A rape, people say, is the act of forcing someone to have sexual intercourse against her will, thus a rape is an aggression on the person. In many cases, even in conjugal life, lovemaking is close to rape due to the uncontrolled excitement and lack of consideration for the partner. Expressing one's lust is called lovemaking. We know very well after the so-called act of lovemaking how frustrated one is. If the sexual act could produce love, then love would be omnipresent and there would be practically no divorce.

What we call lovemaking is nothing but the instinct of mating for the purpose of procreation. Yes, if it is properly studied and understood, then it can open the door towards love. People are so frustrated with sex that they have invented pornography, indulged in homosexuality, paedophilia, adultery and so many other vices related to sex. Yet they call it love.

Real love is divine. It is a very pure state of both cosmic and individual life. It can be experienced only when one has transcended lust, obsession and greed. When love starts blossoming in an individual, it indicates that the person is growing and becoming mature. This does not mean that a person who has known love cannot have sex. However, such an individual has known something far more beautiful. Love brings a great revolution in one's life. With its dawn, compassion, forgiveness, sharing, freedom and awareness are born. I have added awareness here to make people realize that love is not blind. The real sense of justice and good judgement comes only when one grows in love.

Marriage, if really understood and properly lived, can open the door to love. Two individuals can help each other to know love. When love is born, they are no longer husband and wife, but simply friends and co-travellers on the path towards the ultimate union. Here I would like to expound on some extracts from the book 'The Prophet' of Khalil Gibran. Therein, the author beautifully summarises the true nature of marriage and love.

"You were born together and you shall be forevermore." The meaning is that man and woman were both created by God and they will always be together. Further he says, "But let there be spaces between your togetherness. And let the winds of heavens dance between you." Man and woman can be together; nevertheless they should conserve each other's freedom. When there is attachment and possessiveness, then there is no space and when space is absent, the silent vibrations of Godliness are also absent.

"Love one another but make not a bond of love." People think that love is a bondage, an attachment between two people, how wrong! Khalil Gibran says, "Let it be rather a moving sea between the shores of your soul." This means love makes one become vast like the sea, yet one conserves one's freedom. In other words, one is not bound by the feelings of the other, nor does one try to bind the other to oneself.

In the same book, we read, "Then said Almitra, 'Speak to us of love.' And he raised his head and looked upon the people, and there fell a stillness upon them. And with a great voice he said, 'When love beckons to you, follow him ....'" Before going into the love sutra of Gibran, let us reflect on this part: 'he raised his head and looked upon the people and there fell a stillness upon them.' No wonder the title of the book is 'The Prophet.' The man, that is, the prophet must have been an enlightened being for such words of wisdom can flow only from a God-realised soul. He by whose look one can experience stillness is no doubt a realized soul. And the people must have been very attentive and open. The word stillness is very important. Love can flourish only in the stillness of mind and heart. The words of the prophet were being sown in the heart of the people whose minds and hearts were still. In fact, they were blessed by the prophet. Today few people can receive blessing, though most people ask for it.

"When love beckons to you, follow him though his ways are hard and steep." In other words, walk on the path of love, but remember that this path is hard and steep. All those who have walked on this path have faced many difficulties, not because of love itself but because of the ego, because of the stupid people around who do not know anything about love and righteousness. Without love, one cannot enjoy life. One cannot sing, dance, play and share. The path of love is the path of the forest where there are innumerable risks. Yet there are also beautiful flowers with fragrance, trees offering shade, waterfalls, rivers, wonderful animals, lush vegetation and the vibrancy of life. Therefore the prophet says to follow the path of love.

"For even as love crowns you, so shall he crucify you. Even as he is for your growth, so is he for your pruning," says the prophet. Love is the ultimate summit, the final crowning. Attaining love, one has achieved everything. The ultimate bliss, power and glory is love, but to attain it the ego must die and the ego dies hard. It has to be hit very hard many times. This is why it is said, "So shall he crucify you ..., so is he for your pruning."

The ego is the root of the artificial man and his pseudo love. For genuine love to be born, the illusive man must die. On the path of love, there are many tests that will shake the ego to its roots. Hence the saying of the prophet, "So shall he descend to your roots and shake them in their clinging to the earth." Here earth means the body, which is made from earth. The ego is very much attached to the body. With the dawn of love, detachment from the body becomes natural and unavoidable. Love is invisible and bodiless (*anang*).

"Like sheaves of corn he gathers you unto himself." That is, he makes you become a whole. Love makes man holy by making him become a whole. Only the whole is holy. Those who have known love are undivided, their heart, mind, body and soul being one. People are in conflict with themselves because the heart and the mind are not in harmony. The body wants lust; the heart seeks love while the mind is bent on reasoning.

But with the dawn of love, "He threshes you to make you naked." Love brings humility and when one is humble, one becomes innocent and childlike. A child is transparent; he does not hide his real nature. He is as he is. Here it is important to understand that the prophet is talking about the journey of the individual soul through the path of love to the Supreme. When he says, "He threshes you ... ," he means that circumstances will come to you so that you can learn to be as you are, and not be a hypocrite. In other words, you will learn to be simple, natural and spontaneous.

Further, the prophet says, "He sifts you to free you from your husks." If you are on the path of righteousness and love and you are willing to learn, you will have the opportunity to be cleansed of your animal and human natures. For example, if you are arrogant, you will learn how to stoop so that your ego is shaken and thus you become humble. By 'husks', he means the countless conditionings that we carry in our mind and heart. People talk about love, but how many are ready to be grinded so that they can become 'white' in mind and heart? They expect only comfort, security and benefits, they do not think of any sacrifice from their part. Before love blossoms, one has to pass through many fires. "He grinds you to whiteness," says the prophet.

Many a time, we are forced to bow down before the force of circumstances. Even the most arrogant persons have to bow when nature turns against them. Thus the prophet says, "He kneads until you are pliant." Love knows no rigidity, no fixation; it is fluid and moves according to the moment. "Love gives naught but itself and takes naught but from itself." Love is already a blessing, what can it give if not itself? Is there anything purer, better, greater, more glorious and marvellous than love? Is there anything more powerful than love? Love gives itself. Why does the prophet say that it takes from itself? Because for love there is no other, there is only one.

"Love possesses not, nor would it be possessed, for love is sufficient unto love." Love is not dependant, therefore it does not have the desire to possess; it is sufficient unto itself. Why do people want to possess? Why do they get attached? Because they are empty.

Today's marriages and so-called love affairs are nothing but stories of possessing and being possessed. How far away people are from the ideals of marriage and love as laid down by Khalil Gibran! It is said that marriage is a legalized form of prostitution, but I say it is more than that both in its sacredness and superficiality. It is superficial because of ignorant people and sacred if it is a path taken by two compatible souls with the aim of helping each other to attain the apex of life.

It has been said that man and woman are only halves. Unfortunately, this truth has been misinterpreted and has reduced us to slaves because we have been made to believe that we are incomplete without a partner. Consequently, marriage has become an obligation. Why do people marry after all? Almost everyone says that he/she is in love and that is why he/she is getting married. This clearly demonstrates that people are completely ignorant about love. Jesus was a celibate. Does it mean that he was devoid of love?

People call marriage a sacred bond, but looking around, it does not seem to be the case. Today's marriage, like many other things, is a program that unfolds and takes form at a given moment. Then the program is quickly infected by the viruses of hatred, jealousy, possessiveness, boredom, infidelity and the like. However, marriage resulting from understanding between compatible partners is definitely a sacred bond.

Love Marriage and Arranged Marriage

Something very strange has happened to us. Since millennia, we use the word love in all parts of the world. Poems, letters, books, songs, talks, discourses, debates and so on about love abound, yet the world is full of violence, hatred, misery, fascism, fanaticism, racism and innumerable evils. Is this not weird? Have we not fallen prey to a great delusion? Are we not doing something else under the name of love? Experience and the current world situation prove that such is the situation. We have gone very far away from love. My observation is that most people do not know what love is. Very few have tasted a little of it.

What do people refer to when they talk of love? Sex, marriage, attachment, infatuation, co-habitation, friendship, but we have already seen that these do not make sense! Scientists say that there is a love centre in the brain, and what we call love is nothing but the reaction of chemicals in our brain and body. Two areas in the brain lay in the cerebral cortex, the more advanced part of the brain. These are the medial insula, which is thought to be responsible for a variety of emotional functions and 'gut feelings' and part of the anterior cingulate, which is known to respond to euphoria-inducing drugs. This research explains why when we are 'in love', we are often in a euphoric state and do not feel depressed.

The American anthropologist, Dr Helen Fisher of Rutgers University of New Jersey, has been carrying out pioneering work using brain scans in order to locate the position of 'love' in the brain. Though her research is still at a preliminary stage, it has been found that there are three types of emotions in the brain: lust, infatuation and attachment. Each emotion has its own specific brain chemistry, which activates the brain when the person is attracted to someone. It seems that nature has provided us with these in order to assure the propagation of our species by activating the vital functions of our body like having sex for procreation and coming together to protect and help the growth of the young child. Close observation will reveal that what people call love is a physical or emotional attraction. There is certainly a mental calculation, especially when it comes to marriage.

Lust is physical attraction. Without it, procreation would not exist, for who would come together if the interest for sex is absent? How many people would care to marry if it were not for sex? In the Bhagavad-Gita, Krishna says, "I am the sexual desire in man for the procreation of mankind, not in conflict with scriptural injunction." This means that nature has put lust in man for procreation, but we should not stop with it. In other words, we should not be obsessed with it. Unfortunately, this is what has happened. We have got obsessed with lust and whenever we become obsessed with something, we miss a higher purpose. Here we miss the possibility of transcending lust to experience love, which is not the release of chemicals that make us become euphoric, but something more subtle, lively and supra-sensual.

Infatuation, says Fisher, makes you focus on the positive qualities of the loved one and ignore the latter's bad habits or traits. This is why many people fall in love with one another and can stay together despite the fact that they know the other is filled with many negative characteristics. People cannot understand why lovers blindly jump into the fire despite being cautioned. Now we know it is all lust and infatuation. However, when the harsh realities of life come forward, the result is quarrel, separation and divorce. Next comes attachment. By the time reality is unveiled and comes to the view of the partners, attachment has already crept in. This is further strengthened by the coming of children. This is why it is advisable to wait for some time before having children in married life. Infatuation and lust between two sane persons do not last long. Attachment can, unless the reality that hits the couple is indeed very hard.

Now that we have understood the reality of what people call love, it is not difficult to understand the so-called love marriage. The same love marriage becomes a compromise or even a hell and often leads to divorce. If what people call love marriage was really so, then the world would be filled with angels today for love can only beget love. However, a look around us shows that one is very far from such a reality. People often refer to their children as 'the fruit of love.' Were Hitler, Genghis Khan and the like the fruit of love too? Love is a blessing that is very deep beyond the heart and the mind. It is something of indescribable beauty and fragrance. In fact, it is bliss, fragrance and beauty. It overflows when one has gone beyond lust, infatuation and attachment. Nay, it happens only when the mind and the heart are transcended. It is the juice of life, the essence of man, independent, free and boundless. How far away man is from it!

Few have tasted love. It can be achieved only when the individual is not. This means that in order to know love, one has to die and be born anew. The ego has to die, like the seed that dies when the plant germinates. It passes through the vicissitudes of life, then flowers, emanates fragrance and finally gives fruits. Love will come first, followed by the perfume, then by the fruits. There is a whole art to this – it is the art of dying. But who is ready to die such a death? Everyone is concerned with marriage, procreation, attachment, progress, competition, who cares to know about love? The saddest part is that very few indeed know about what I have mentioned. Therefore, know that such a thing as love marriage does not exist. Love has nothing to do with marriage. It rather has to do with evolution of the person. Yes, those who have attained it can choose to come together, but then it will be a totally different kind of relationship.

Now let us turn to what people call arranged marriage. But before this, I would like to make it clear that I am not against lust, infatuation, attachment and even marriage as these are opportunities or doors. I will even venture to say that these can be doors to the ultimate possibility of life. However, by dwelling on them or by being carried away by them, we fail to move higher.

Even what we call arranged marriage is motivated by lust, infatuation and attraction, which eventually lead to attachment and obsession. Here the partners' meeting is arranged by their relatives or friends. Rarely do they get attracted spontaneously to each other, instead their relationship develops gradually. In these cases, the object of lust has not been achieved yet, therefore it is arranged for. There may be a mismatch, but attachment bonds the couple together or there is a compromise.

In many cases, strong pressure from parents, particularly on girls, leads to an arranged marriage. In such cases, I would advise the young people not to give in to pressure, but to fight back as nobody is the possession of anyone. You have your own individuality. Neither morally, nor legally can any member of society force you to get married. Many parents simply encourage their children to jump in married life and when things fall apart, they complain and shift the guilt on destiny or blame others. They themselves are ignorant and most of the time, are a victim of society and their own ignorance. Hence they cannot properly guide their children towards a sound married life. Marriage should be a conscious and intelligent choice. If you intend to lead a family life, first study objectively the realities of married life, otherwise you may bitterly regret your decision.

While in love marriages partners get attracted to each other due to biological, chemical or psychological compatibilities, in arranged marriages the coming together is due to a social arrangement. But even then, lust, attraction and infatuation are present in the partners; otherwise it will be a forced marriage. This can happen but is very rare. Absence of lust, infatuation or attraction does not necessarily imply transcendence. Some people simply stagnate or vegetate; they are barren. They simply move about like a corpse, their life is mechanical or animal-like. Even animals have an important role to play in evolution, but such people are as good as dead.

Many people marry but have no satisfaction on the sexual and family levels and thus have no motivation or aim in life. People say that arranged marriage lasts longer in most cases. It may be so because initially there was not much hope, expectation or fantasy about the partner. But this does not mean that it is better because those who go through an arranged marriage have their dreams too, though they may not be as sweet as those who 'fall in love'.

Though people marry because of tradition, fear, habit, lust, infatuation and other such reasons, the truth is that evolution has its hand in it. We are driven by the evolutionary force, though of course, we are free not to get drowned by it and use it instead for our growth. However, it is a question of freedom of mind and few people know about such freedom. Hence, whether it is a love marriage or an arranged one, the fundamental realities are the same. Still, I would prefer love marriage to arranged one, as it is more natural. But the end result is more or less the same, with the exception that in love marriage, there is more disappointment and frustration that can lead to separation more easily. Such a situation is important to make people realize that what they call love is like running after a mirage in the desert.

Courtship and After Marriage

It is usually said that courtship is better than marriage and some even believe it to be the best moment of life. It may not necessarily be so, but it is certainly better than marriage. It is also said that love diminishes with marriage. But then, it cannot really be love, otherwise it would not decrease. Before marriage, one has not yet become the other one's property, therefore there is some liberty and the relationship stands good. For love to flourish, freedom is of paramount importance.

Before marriage, there is no responsibility and it is all pleasure. Whenever one meets the other, it is for chatting, going out, love making and the like. After marriage, one knows that the other is here, so why be in a hurry. One can have the other at any time, therefore closeness is lost. During courtship, however, one has to make the best of the moment because after some time, there will be separation and at times it is for quite long. This is a period when one has to prove oneself, therefore one will strive to wear the best mask in every way, by dressing smartly, showing good manners, behaving nicely and so on. Only after marriage will the real face reveal itself. In some cases, partners have not known each other intimately during courtship. Thus the curiosity and desire are still there after marriage, resulting in an attraction, though this too gradually disappears.

Pre-marital attitudes vary widely. In general, courtship is paradise-like. It is a world of fantasy and dreams; projects of marriage are discussed with much passion. In some cases, young partners quarrel over trivia, then reconcile quickly and this happens very often. It is sad to note that even after spending years together, boys and girls fail to know and understand each other. While marriage should be based on understanding and love, there should be some basic agreements. For example, one partner may not like to become a parent soon after marriage, while the other may be in a hurry for that. A compromise should be reached and matters should be discussed very frankly. Unfortunately, few people discuss such important issues before marriage mainly due to lack of maturity, but often to avoid deep reflection and discussion, which may end up in a quarrel or even split.

It is equally true that before marriage, many people think that married life is a constant honeymoon or love affair and courtship days are only to be enjoyed, not to be spent on serious reflection. However, it does not take long to realize that such is not the case. And when they are awakened to the bitter reality, they say, "If I had known, I would not have got married," or "I regret that I got married at such a young age." I consider it unwise to reach such a state of affairs. People do not learn their lessons. Most of the time people go into marriage without themselves having reached intellectual maturity or having acquired a solid material base. It is always a question of 'I will manage it.'

After marriage, the flame becomes dimmer and dimmer and in many cases even goes out. After one or two children, the excitement or the adventure is no more. Sex, love, affection, going out and the company of one another become routine. There is a saying that goes like this, "Too much of anything becomes boring." This is true to a great extent for almost everything, particularly marriage. It is very rare that after marriage there is the same flame of love and passion. It is the same lust, but it fades away with time for the partner.

There do exist some rare couples who experience love, closeness and help each other even after marriage, but these are exceptions. In most cases, there is disillusionment. The expectations and hopes are lost, the image that one had in mind does not materialize. In short, it is all a shattered dream. In the beginning, married life is still not bad in many cases, but as days pass by and the masks fall off, it becomes unbearable and both partners' lives become hellish. Initially, one would sing, "She wears my ring ...," then it becomes, "Give me back my ring ...!"

People do not know how to live the pre-marital period. There is too much blind bondage that does not allow learning anything about the partner. Some become physically so intimate before marriage that afterwards the curiosity and desire die, hence one wants to have new adventures. Today, many persons live together with their partners even before marriage. Consequently, being together after marriage is already an old affair that is no more pleasurable, thus the need for new conquests.

It has been observed that before marriage, precisely during courtship, lovers, especially girls lose weight, they eat less and even sleep less. People often make jokes about this, but it can be explained. After marriage, it is the contrary as couples tend to put on weight. The reason is that with the feeling of love and sex, the first two lower *chakras* (centres of energy) become activated a little. The first centre is related to sex and the second one to emotion. Being unconsciously fuelled with the energy of sex and feeling, they do not feel the need for food.

After marriage, however, sex is a routine, while feeling becomes gross and even disappears. They are replaced by food, hence the reason for putting on weight. These two lower centres are related to two higher ones. The sex centre or the *muladhara* is related to the heart *chakra*, which is the cosmic love *chakra*. Sex is gross and is lust, while love is subtle and is the other side of the coin. The second one, the emotional centre, is related to the throat centre. Here the sweetness of emotion becomes the nectar of immortality. If a married life is a spiritual one, then one's consciousness moves from the lower centres to the higher ones.

Love is experienced when lust, feelings and the animalistic and human natures are transcended. At the fourth *chakra*, cosmic love is experienced. It is not a body-to-body or heart-to-heart affair, but a oneness that encompasses the whole existence. Those who stick to body consciousness or the emotional body do not reach the *anahata chakra*, as the fourth centre is also called. By living a conjugal life as is commonly done, by indulging too much in sex or by getting obsessed by emotions, one loses the possibility of experiencing love and immortality.

Psychology says that every man seeks his mother in his wife and every woman her father in her husband. When the image fits, then it is a good combination and married life goes on fairly well, otherwise it is chaotic. And since this rarely happens, as it is nearly impossible to find the image of one's father or mother in another person, things do not work. Why do men like the breasts of women? And why does a woman hold the head of a man when the latter is making love to her? It is a very subtle mother and child relationship. It is a child who sucks the breast. And it is very natural for a woman to find a child in her husband. These are mostly unconscious realities and this is why many people may not agree with them.

Most conjugal relationships stop at husband and wife level, while there could be other dimensions of a man and a woman's relationship. Why can it not be a friend-friend relationship? Or a mother and son or father and daughter relationship? It could also be a co-traveller relationship. Most couples do not go through these experiences as life turns into a nightmare. However, sticking to any of these is a sign of stagnancy. One should keep on moving because ultimately one is alone, without any relationship whatsoever. Nowadays, the very concept of marriage makes a boring and conflicting conjugal life. After a certain period, one feels as if one is carrying a burden.

Sexuality

A man and a woman do not become husband and wife by simply signing the marriage contract or performing the rites of marriage. The relationship of husband and wife slowly develops as understanding and love grow between two compatible persons of opposite sex who decide to take the journey of life together. Spiritual evolution of husband and wife is possible only when there is total openness between the partners. Thus all barriers are broken, leading to a sharing and mergence of the opposite forces. But this is very rare indeed as people are very possessive and when there is possessiveness, it is not possible to open to one another.

From duality, unity can be born. Likewise between man and woman, oneness can be born, as symbolised by the image of Ardhanareswar in the Hindu religion. However, man or woman should seek the right partner so that they can meet at the most intimate level. The sexual relationship is the highest intimacy and contact so far as the body is concerned. For the heart, love is a higher level of intimacy and *samadhi* is the ultimate union so far as the soul is concerned. At the last stage, there is only one, not two. The child is both the mother and the father and at the same time it is neither. Similarly, love is both male and female and also neither. But love is born when both maleness and feminineness annihilate each other in a mutual contact at a very high level of meditation. And meditation is born with learning, sacrifice and practice of the right way of living.

The most sacred thing is not always exposed; it is almost hidden and at times invisible. God is the most sacred of all and is invisible. Normally, sexual union is sacred as it is the means to procreate, but we have degraded it by disrespecting it in various ways such as by doing it at times in public places. When the Lord created the universe, nobody was there. The seed germinates in the dark recesses of the soil. Countless events occurring on the microscopic as well as the macroscopic levels are hidden, invisible, non-profane and hence sacred. Similarly, the sexual organ is not exposed to the eyes of one and all.

Sex is the source of love and life and on the macroscopic level, it is the base of the whole existence. Yet such a sacred thing has been turned into a taboo – why? Maybe because it is the power that will make man a god. Mystics say that the sexual energy can be transformed and this can lead man to have a highly developed mind, so much so that the sexual energy can contribute to lead man to attain cosmic consciousness. Therefore it seems normal for society to kill this possibility that will create a free man, not a slave. Man can be commanded only when he is weak, and he is so weak so far as sex is concerned that he is easily manipulated.

In my opinion, the taboo around sex has been created to retain man in such a stagnant state that his spiritual quest is blocked. But this cunningness and sin cannot last for long. One day will come when man's understanding of sex will grow so much that he will no longer be a slave to it. This wisdom will move his energy upward and will make him an illumined being. He will have enough fuel to make his mind stay in a state of constant awakening. That will be the day of real celebration, for it is only when one is free that one can celebrate.

The human being is the greatest miracle-maker. Every problem is created by us and the solution too rests in our hands. Man is sexual from head to toe, yet he wants to escape from it when the subject comes on the table. Every cell of our body has been made from sexual energy and sexual orgasm. Pleasure is fundamentally the same, but through the sexual contact, one touches such an intensity and subtlety of pleasure that we are irresistibly drawn towards it. The big question mark persists though we have reached considerable height in scientific researches. Mystics, however, have gone very deep into the subject to discover the secret that lies behind the appearance.

In the East, they have even devised methods, known as *tantra*, so as to go deep into sex in order to have a greater understanding. The mystics say that the pleasure achieved through sexual union is basically divine. A glimpse of God is tasted when the sexual act reaches the ultimate point called coitus. Said in another way, through sexual intercourse, one can peep through eternity for a split second. Our sexual energy is produced from food, the intake of oxygen, sunlight and the mind. One human cell from a male and another one from a female unite to give birth to a human being. Their meeting at the physical level releases energy from both sides. Therefore, we meet on a gross level, then on a subtle one. The gross level is bodily embrace while the subtle level is the love that is shared. Furthermore, the vital fluid and the sperm, which are the essence of the man, and the ovum, which is the vitality of the woman, meet too – that is the subtle union.

However, the meeting is so momentary that we hardly feel the pleasure of a deep union. It is one of the most fundamental reasons why we are so obsessed by it. In this context, the woman is more fortunate because her orgasm is more profound and expansive. But most of the time, she does not reach such a height as most partners do not know the art of lovemaking. Also, many women cannot reach a deep orgasm due to certain factors.

While man's orgasm is very shallow and stops at the head of his sexual organ, woman's orgasm is spread all over, probably because she has erogenous zones located in several parts of her body. A woman's orgasm is enjoyed with eyes closed, like in meditation. In such a state, she 'interiorises' the pleasure that thus becomes more intense. On the other hand, man is extrovert and is curious to know how his partner is reacting. Therefore we see that there are many differences between man's and woman's sexuality. Though male and female bodies are made in such a way that they can come together, man and woman are different. This is why it is good to choose one's partner carefully if we wish to be compatible in life, have the best progeny and progress spiritually.

If instead of having adequate meals, we eat very little, then we will want food every now and then. It will become a habit.

Nowadays sex has become a bad habit and is done with a sense of guilt. When there is much love between the partners, then the moment of pleasure increases and one becomes less obsessed by it. The result is that the energy starts moving upwards. In fact, the purpose of sexual energy is to procreate and to act as fuel for meditation. Actually, we procreate and waste the rest of the energy in habit and obsession. Through meditation, one can have much more joy of the same quality and that joy can be increased to such an extent so as to create an explosion of our being. Such an explosion is called *samadhi* in the East, which can be translated as cosmic consciousness.

Man is a strange being: he toils a lot to feed himself, then the energy he has produced is thrown out as waste by a moment of excitation. An iota of the energy can produce a complete human being who could be an Einstein, a Vivekananda, a Jesus or a Krishna! What will be the outcome if the whole potential is transformed? Both man and woman possess male and female aspects. Their union is meant to produce the union of the inner man and woman without depending on each other on a bodily basis to attain the same orgasm as in sexual union. Marriage was meant to be a mutual consent between two persons of the same level of vibration so as to help each other to attain oneness with the Whole, by uniting the inner male and female principles or by uniting the positive and negative poles.

The sexual union is the merging of positive and negative and also the complementary elements of nature for the evolution of life. When union occurs at the gross level, procreation is the result. When the meeting is subtle, illumination is the result. Darkness-light, matter-energy, male-female are opposite but complementary aspects upon whose basis the drama of creation is being played. God is in an eternal, infinitely subtle 'sexual intercourse' in the form of matter-energy, Satti-Shiva, darkness-light. This is the reason why the process of creation is eternal.

The sexual energy should be saved and transformed so as to attain the apex of joy, which frees one from all forms of suffering. This, however, does not mean sexual repression. One has to go through it, know it deeply and then transcend it. Sexual union is the first rung on the ladder of spiritual evolution. The ultimate rung is enlightenment. Without proper sex education, no religious or spiritual evolution is possible. As the sexual fluid is gradually transformed, the mind becomes powerful and pure. Geniuses can be produced in greater numbers if the sexual energy is transformed.

Meditation is the only science that can bring about this transformation and it should start at the age of puberty when the sex centre starts operating. Sexual intercourse should be for procreation and experience of bliss and thus Divinity. One should not be a slave to it. Sexual relation nowadays amounts to sneezing. In our actual civilisation, sex has become such a problem that one feels like carrying a burden and one is always seeking an opportunity to unload oneself from it.

Sex-based Marriages

Many people marry to enjoy sex freely and legally. When it is found that going into sex without getting married or having it with different partners is immoral, then marriage is used as a suitable solution to camouflage the sexual affair. Today we read in the newspapers that a husband has raped his wife. This seems strange yet it is true. When a marriage is based on sex, problems are bound to crop up because very rarely does sex bring full satisfaction.

People do not know how to approach their partner. Many do not even know how to perform the sexual act correctly. How many people understand the sexuality of the opposite sex well? I have addressed these issues in my book 'Sex, Breaking the Taboo', which gives a better understanding of the subject. Making women an object of sexual desire is very ugly indeed and terribly offending to them. They feel they are being used. It is said that women give sex to have love while men give love to have sex. This is a business and once again love is absent. Where there is love, there is sharing, not business. Sex should be a by-product of love.

If there is too much indulgence before marriage, then one may not have much pleasure in sex after marriage. It is a choice that one has to make. This is more a man's problem as they indulge much more in masturbation and sexual relationship than women. But that is also true that expecting total satisfaction in sex is an illusion. It is like a fire that is inflamed by adding more fuel to it. Here I am reminded of the story of Yayati from the Mahabharata. He was a king who wanted to enjoy sex as long as he wished, but he had been cursed to lose his youth. However, there was a condition attached that he could exchange his old age for a youthful life if any of his sons were willing to accept it. All of them refused, except the youngest one. So Yayati became young again and indulged in sex for a very long time. But the more he enjoyed it, the more his desire kept growing, until finally he got tired of it. He then realised that it was not possible to be completely satisfied with sex and resumed his old age.

Some men would not accept to marry a non-virgin girl, as if virginity is the most important thing in a woman. Should not women too question the virginity of men? Why should it be one-sided? Many men take the virginity of girls and then leave them without thinking that one day those girls will get married and perhaps come across stupid guys like them. Also, many girls go out with lovers and lose their virginity before marriage. Later, they invent a pretext to fool their husbands. How can there be love in such couples where there is no trust and frankness?

When it comes to sex, there should not be any feeling of guilt or shame between partners. It should be faced with full acceptance. I recommend the study of the Kama Sutra, which was written not by a pervert but by a sage. It was written with the view to help people attain maximum satisfaction so that transcendence becomes possible because without transcendence meditation cannot happen.

Those who make sex the main objective of marriage are very far from what a married life should be. I know of people who, when their partner decline to have sex, retort: "Why did I marry you?" or "Shall I seek it from others?" Then the following questions arise. Can we not abstain from it for one or a few days? Is the relationship only sexual? If it were not for sex, would people get married? There is also another side of the coin. Should we deprive our partner of such a great pleasure for long? How often should we go into sex? Some partners, mostly male, want anal penetration. Should this be accepted? Is this natural?

All these questions create conflicts in conjugal life and cannot be dealt with lightly. It is not a matter of opinion because anyone can have his own opinion. One must differentiate between an opinion and the truth about any matter. Opinions are numerous and vary according to the character of each person, while the reality is known only by the wise. Therefore there should not be blind acceptance of the partner's opinion. Some people's honeymoon or the first night is like a rape. Such aggressiveness and violence at the very beginning of conjugal life are not signs of love and comprehension. When sex is simply reduced to a mere release of one's energy without bothering about the pleasure of the other, how can love and compassion thrive?

I have mentioned in my book, 'Sex, Breaking the Taboo', that women have more than one orgasm at a time and may obviously feel incomplete and frustrated with only one or two orgasms. Few men realise this. The question that arises then is, for how long can a woman bear this situation and remain faithful to her partner without suppressing it? Of course, the problem will not arise if one has already embarked on the spiritual path under the guidance of a spiritual master. One will then use the sexual energy to fuel the expansion of the mind. A very comprehensive and frank discussion is important on the subject of sex before the start of married life. There should not be the least hesitation to consider the advice of an expert on the matter.

Most people think they know too much on the subject and therefore feel much offended when they are advised to learn more concerning sex. Many men think that if they can have more than one ejaculation per day, then they are experts in the field. In this context I think animals can do better. They can even have longer orgasms than human beings. The truth of sex is deeper than the duration or the number of orgasms one can have. Remember that life starts with sex. Therefore, one should be very careful about it. It should be given much consideration. Otherwise we may find ourselves in very complex situations. It will be very unwise and sad if a marriage fails because of a wrong notion or ignorance about such a sacred art.

Knowing the Basic Differences between Man and Woman

No two things are equal in the whole existence – each particle has its uniqueness. Both man and woman have a unique position in this universal drama. However, it must be understood that both of them have fundamental differences. To be able to give either of them their respective place in the march towards both material and spiritual evolution, an overall understanding of the inner and outer life of both man and woman is essential. And such wisdom lies only in the heart of the enlightened one. Occult knowledge of both feminine and masculine psyche is of paramount importance, for only this will make one understand that man and woman are not equal, but are divine potentials that can be unfolded by using their own natural tendencies.

Many have tried to prove that man and woman are equal. When this failed, they started to talk about equal rights. Equal rights seem a better deal. Woman is God's or nature's heart while man is His mind. This does not mean that woman is not mind at all or man is not heart at all. But one aspect predominates in one gender, thus the full feminine nature of God manifests through woman, while man displays His male nature. This is why there is maleness and feminineness. In a body, both heart and mind are present, therefore in one body there are both male and female possibilities. By coming together, each partner can help the other to manifest the virtue of the predominating factor (heart or mind).

The heart is the heart and is very different from the mind. Love is one thing and consciousness is another, though both are aspects of one reality. Similarly, man and woman are different and this makes the richness of human and even animal species. Both man and woman have qualities that can be used to attain God. Let us go into their basic differences and marvel at their nature. It is as if nature has built two separate parts that have to be put together to produce a given reality. Unfortunately, human intelligence has stopped at such a low level that the opposite sexes come together solely to produce children and to generate conflicts.

The first difference is at the physical level. Man's and woman's bodies are different in many respects. I would like to start with the sexual differences. Man's sperm is very small in comparison to the ovum. The latter is powerful, but static and receptive, while the sperm, though powerful too, is aggressive, competitive and active. The sperm represents energy while the ovum represents matter. The latter is like the earth, which is there expecting the forces of the sky to fecundate it. One egg is surrounded by millions of sperms, but only one is accepted on board. This gives an insight into the monogamous nature of woman. However, there are always exceptions, thus the ovum may at times accept two or more sperms, then break apart forming two or more zygotes.

Women have a womb, which is the cradle of life. Both man and woman are formed in the womb of a woman. The fact that every male spends his first nine months in the womb of a woman gives man an inferiority complex. Mothers have a very special place in human life and this adds to the inferiority complex of men as fathers. Man and woman perceive the world differently. Studies of the brain's structure have shown that there are significant differences between men and women. Men's brains are on the average 15% larger than women's, although this can be related to their larger body size. On the other hand, women's brains are more densely populated with neurones.

Research has shown that a man tends to use one side of the brain at a time, while a woman more often uses both sides of the brain. The structure of a woman's brain supports this fact, as it has a much larger *corpus callosum* than man's brain. This is probably why it is believed that there is much more communication between the two hemispheres of a woman's brain than is possible in a man's.

It is now a scientific fact that there are subtle differences in the way the brains of men and women process language, information, emotion, cognition and others. It is interesting to note that men and women estimate time, judge the speed of things, carry out mental calculations, orient in space and visualise objects in three dimensions and so on differently. Science says that in all these tasks men and women are strikingly different. This may account for the fact that there are more male mathematicians, airplane pilots, bus guides, mechanical engineers, architects and car-race drivers than female ones.

A woman's body is more delicate, sensitive to touch and receptive, thus when it comes to prayer, worship, fasting and devotion, she excels. However, when it comes to meditation, which is a mind affair, man excels. Meditation is an affair of willpower, thus of mind, while prayer, worship and the like are a matter of faith, thus of the heart. Women are more inclined towards the heart than men; they are more intuitive and psychically developed than men. It is as if their senses are more delicate than those of men. Men's bodies are more solid as they have bigger muscles, nerves and bones. This clearly demonstrates that nature has built them to do harder works and severe austerities. This does not mean that women cannot do likewise, but their bodies are meant for practices like devotion and for light works.

Let us consider other differences. Women's eyes have a larger white area than men's because close-range personal communication is an integral part of female behaviour. And a larger white area allows a greater range of eye signal to be sent and received in the direction the eyes move. Many women's peripheral vision is effective up to almost 180°. In other words, women have a short but wide range vision. For instance, she may notice a hair on a person's collar and even recognise it to be that of a woman, but will have much difficulty in parking the car in the garage. Men, however, see narrow and far away. Such differences have always been the cause of conflict in couples. A man may, for example, fail to understand why women cannot drive as well as men at night. The reason is that men's vision is long-range while women's is short-range.

Since vision is a brain affair and the brain is an instrument of the mind, the way men and women see the world is also different. A woman's environment is immediate with herself, children, house, husband, parents, in-laws and so on. Man, on the other hand, has a far away vision; he thinks of colonizing the planets, climbing the Everest and the like. Intuition, love, poetry, endurance, motherliness, forgiveness, patience, shyness, softness and many other qualities are feminine virtues. They are found both in men and women, but they manifest more naturally in women. On the other hand, reasoning faculty, adventure, aggressiveness, physical power, ambition and the like are equally present in both genders, but they are male qualities. A complete, harmonious and successful life is not possible without both male and female qualities. Marriage represents an agreement for the union of these powers for the evolution of both genders on the spiritual and material levels. However, mutuality should be the basis of such an agreement; otherwise things will certainly go wrong.

Whatever be the differences between the sexes, they were brought about by nature, thus should not be the cause of conflict between them. These differences are scientific; they do not stem from a mind that is against either of them and their evolution. In my mind and in truth, woman is God's reflection as much as man. Each one has his or her own special characteristics. Their material evolution as well as their spiritual growth can best unfold along their own line. By this, I mean both can evolve by understanding and accepting their nature, not by denying it.

Today it is sad to see that women want to prove that they are as good as men in almost all fields. In so doing, they are losing something extremely precious. However, this can be understood and the responsibility rests on the shoulder of men who for so many centuries have oppressed and dominated them. But it should not be an opportunity for women to go to the other extreme. There is much they can gain by revolting against men's oppression, but at the same time they should realize that they are women and that through them God is seeking to manifest something extremely beautiful and unparalleled.

Man and woman are much more than mere physical beings and the stability of a married couple and the base of a sane relationship depends a lot on the knowledge of their psychic layers. Today our knowledge of the human being is nothing more than that of the tip of the iceberg. Likes repel and opposites attract, therefore man and woman attract each other. This attraction is powerful and irresistible like that between a needle and a magnet. It is the root cause of conflict and also the lure of sex and marriage. Without it, man and woman would probably not come together, nor form a family or bear children.

Because of this great attraction, there is also a lot of frustration. On one hand, they cannot live without each other and on the other, when they come together they make a hell out of their union. The blunt truth is that we are attracted not only to the person who is our partner, but to others too. This happens not because we are evil as many believe it, but because such is our nature. Not having the right partner also causes one to get attracted to someone else. Meeting the right partner is not the end of married life; in fact, it is only the beginning. The goal is to use it as a means to a higher purpose that will fulfil our being. Till this does not happen, we will go on getting attracted to other individuals.

As man and woman evolve, their consciousness moves from one layer to another. For example, man's consciousness will shift from the first to the second layer, which is female and is the emotional body. This will bring certain changes in him. He will have a few feminine or emotional traits, which are very important for his own evolution, like empathy. It helps one to know or to understand others' suffering or any other feeling. Many such refined qualities of the emotional body can be developed. But if one is not working to undergo a great transformation leading to God-realization, then one may end up developing many gross emotions and feminine qualities, which can impair spiritual and mental growth.

Normally when the emotional body develops in man, the latter retains his male characteristics, though he will be manifesting some feminine traits. Unfortunately, men in general have been taught to suppress feminine characteristics, considering them to be weaknesses. Thus men are deprived from the opportunity to understand women. Lack of awareness and a small deficiency of male hormones can result in a feminine nature in man. In such a context, some men can become homosexuals or transvestites. Some young boys already have a deficiency of the masculine hormone, testosterone, and have been made feminine by the force of circumstances during childhood. For instance, if a couple has given too much care to their daughter and neglected their son, the latter may understand that a girl will always have much more affection and care in life. This notion may unconsciously develop feminine characteristics in him, which will manifest to a high degree when the second body develops.

What we have to understand is that the opposite characteristics within us are gifts from nature. We have to use those traits and then go beyond them while retaining our original nature. This applies to women also, whose second body is male. Unfortunately, due to our ignorance, problems arise when our natural tendencies start to unfold. Human life is a great library where knowledge of man, God and the universe is concealed. It is only when one is ready to learn, casting aside one's arrogance and conditionings, that one can know the truth therein. This is why I insist on the motto 'Know Thyself.' The Upanishads rightly say, "Know that by knowing which all else gets known." To know man, woman must study herself fully, and vice versa. Every man carries a woman within. Similarly, every woman carries a man within. A partner of the opposite sex can only help us to unite with our opposite partner inside us. Great study and insight are needed in order to have such knowledge.

We live without the fundamental knowledge of ourselves and thus we meet with much conflict and frustration at all levels. We have nearly everything save self-education. This implies that we have nothing, because what avails a man if he gains the whole world but is ignorant of his own self? Man has made laudable progress in the material field, but has failed lamentably in the area of self or spiritual knowledge. Old married couples believe they have known life, who else can teach them anything? The tragedy is that many people with a modicum of bookish knowledge and little experience in this field are enmeshed by arrogance. They refuse to learn further. These are the blind people and others who know nothing follow them, thus making true the saying of Jesus, "The blind follow the blind and both fall in the ditch."

The Spiritual Couple

A spiritual couple consists of a man and a woman who, out of intelligence, have determined to transcend their animal and human natures to attain the state of Godliness. It is very clear to them that such a realization is possible only by treading the path of truth. They are aware of the fundamental differences between a man and a woman. However, instead of making a conflict out of them, they have understood that it is possible to use them as means in order to attain God-realization. Such persons know fairly well that they are human beings with both weaknesses and good qualities. They have accepted themselves as they are and are striving hard with the help of a genuine master to transcend their lower self. Despite being spiritual aspirants, they do fall and rise, but they know that falling forms part of the lessons of life and therefore learn from each fall. They understand what Gandhi said: "The greatness of a person lies not in his never falling, but in his rise after each fall."

The woman is the negative pole while the man is the positive one. By their coming together, a great force of oneness is developed. Let me give an example to explain how this works. Most of us have heard of matter and anti-matter. When particles of matter and anti-matter come together, they annihilate one another and what is left is radiation, which is neither of them. Similarly, when man and woman come very close in every sense of the word, then both dissolve and a new being is born, which is neither man nor woman. The Indian mystics have called it Ardhanareshwar. This does not imply that they will dissolve physically. The truth is that they will cease to exist as ego, which is the cause of separation, and will realize their oneness with one another and with existence. They will know that they are one soul and that the soul has no gender. This characteristic belongs to the body, the ego, the mind and the heart. With such a realization, a woman becomes a better woman. In fact, she attains the apex of womanhood, which the Hindus have called *devi* (goddess). Similarly, man attains the apex of manhood called *deva* (god).

So that there can be mergence between husband and wife, like matter and anti-matter, there should be total openness between both partners. Both should be pure in body, mind and heart and be on the path of truth, otherwise the explosion will not take place. As I have said, this may seem difficult because of our conditionings. Nevertheless, if we are really determined and prepared to pay the price, then things become less difficult and painful. The practice of *tantra* becomes easy for a spiritual couple. This practice is a means to transcend body consciousness and thus go beyond the mere relationship of husband and wife. They can be just helping partners, also called *tantric* partners. In fact, spiritual couples can be *tantric* partners without having to go through any ritual or formal relationship.

The greatest *tantric* practice between such partners is the transformation of sex or lust into love. Sex is a very powerful drive in human life and until one is liberated from it, meditation is impossible. A couple can bring the energy to the highest bubbling point with a view to transform it. But here it is good to understand that one should be very strong mentally or else one may fall. Of course, there may be many attempts. One must have enjoyed it first without over-wasting the energy; otherwise one may not have enough to bring about the explosion. Any spiritual practice should be carried out under the guidance of a spiritual guide.

Remember that on the spiritual path each partner should evolve according to his or her own nature without imitating one another. Meditation can be practised together, though each one must have one's moment of solitude for deep reflection. During meditation, the wife must be seated at the left of the man as this creates a better vibration. There are certain practices that can be done together, but these have to be taught by a master. Those who want to have quick progress should better have no children as then they will have to focus much energy externally. If however, one partner desires to have one, then it should be decided whether there is really the need to have it. A woman must have a child only when she feels that it will complete her, not because of others' influence as this is wrong.

Spiritual couples do not think that life is to be rejected. On the contrary, it is viewed like a beautiful garden for divine lovers, therefore it is to be enjoyed, but without forgetting the middle path. Spiritual couples are intelligent, energetic, jovial and lovely. Indeed, such a divine partnership is extremely rare, though the potential is in everyone. A spiritual couple is the most natural one, but even for the latter, paradise has been lost. Adam and Eve have been thrown out. They themselves are responsible for it, so they will have to work to win back the lost paradise.

From lust one has to move to love, from mere feeling and emotion one has to move to love. Love neither grieves nor causes grief. It does not bind or possess the other, instead it liberates. Today people think that love implies attachment, jealousy and possessiveness. Man and woman are like two birds caught in a net; only their friendship can help the liberation of each other, not their attachment. Love brings independence. In a love relationship, when one partner falls, the other does his/her best to help the former, not to condemn or to make the other feel guilty.

A couple that grows in intelligence and love can teach their children the same thing. Parents should be facilitators to their children instead of behaving like their owners. When compatible spiritual partners come together, a great force or a whole is created. This is a scientific fact. However, such persons are not born already prepared. They learn the art and evolve in a mystical or a spiritual atmosphere under the guidance of an enlightened being. Spiritual couples are rare though the potential exists in our society. The trouble is that many people do not wish to embark on the adventure of learning and into the unknown. They are happy with their petty dream world. The purity of life of a spiritual couple can produce great miracles. Purity of life means purity in thought, word and deed. Men and women are gods and goddesses in potential, so one can imagine the power that can be engendered if both join forces. Today we are fighting and trying to exert our control over each other and this has led to a totally insane humanity.

The heart and the head are two great sources of power and virtue, each one having its own uniqueness. In this context, both man and woman possess much power and many virtues that can be easily tapped if they come together in love, harmony and intelligence. Each one is the complement of the other and not mere opposites. We were made in such a way so that we can meet at a very fundamental level, but due to our ignorance we are unable to see those points where our beings can meet. We stop only at the physical level and thus miss the most important things. Both the heart and the head are located in the same body. Therefore, they are naturally meant to act in harmony.

Similarly, man and woman are naturally meant to work together for their progress, both material and spiritual. Due to ignorance and misunderstanding, there has been a great chasm between man and woman. Research and learning can bring us together for the welfare of one and all. Presently, the aggressiveness and hostility between them are great and this can be understood. Men are largely responsible for that state of affairs. But shall we spend our time laying the responsibility on them without doing what is right? Is it enough to fight for equal rights socially? Should women not recognize their own nature? Should men not help in that endeavour? We are bound to live in harmony not only socially but also spiritually; otherwise we will have failed as human beings. We will have failed to realize the image of the Divine according to which both have been created.

Some Marriage Ceremonies and their Meanings

Apart from being symbolic, marriage is meant to remind people of a sense of discipline and responsibility that is incumbent on them. For example, to conceive and to bring up a child, two persons cannot come together only for some time to satisfy their lust and be in the company of one another. A great sense of responsibility, commitment, agreement and sharing is of paramount importance.

Men and women are human beings and as such they have weaknesses. Therefore at times, they have to be reminded and helped to enable them to fulfil their responsibilities. Marriage with its many rites and rituals is meant to achieve that purpose. The oaths that are taken should remind us of certain facts. This, however, does not make us super-humans as we can fall at any time. But an oath is always here to remind us that we have agreed to assume certain responsibilities, which can best be fulfilled with the cooperation of our partner. Man should not be guilty of his fall, neither should he keep on doing the same mistake over and over again, which shows that he is not learning his lessons.

Today marriage has been reduced to a social convention while in truth it is much more than that, as we have already discovered. Going into different types of marriage ceremonies, we can have an idea of the responsibility that married life implies. Something that is common in all marriages is the ring. Couples wear a ring around the ring finger. Why a ring and why that particular finger? It is wrongly believed that the ring implies bondage and wearing it means that one is bound forever with the partner. No doubt this interpretation stems from the bitter experience of married life. Couples feel that they have been trapped. But who has trapped whom? If it is a trap, is the one who is trapped not responsible too? However, the truth is that it is an opportunity for learning very important lessons of life.

The ring being a circle is a symbol of oneness. It is worn in that particular finger because it represents the middle path. The little and the forefinger stand for the two extremes of life, or inertia and incessant dynamism (*tamas* and *rajas*), while the ring finger symbolizes the balance, the middle path. It is good to note that the thumb represents the Absolute while the first finger symbolises the ego. That which is in the middle is both and neither, symbolizing both sex and the soul or *atma*, which is the Beyond. Human being has gender but is also beyond it. Oneness with existence is possible when one's inner feminine and masculine natures are united and a person of the opposite sex can be helpful in that endeavour.

In many religions, man wears a ring in the right hand finger while women in the left, symbolizing the union of right and left. It is said that man's left side must unite to woman's right and woman's left side to man's right. Both then form one whole being. This is the reason why in Hindu marriages, the bride is made to stand to the left of the bridegroom. In some communities, this is a main feature while in others there are other more important rites. For example in Islam, taking the name of God and expressing approval of *nikkah* is probably the most important part of the ceremony. It is an oath of acceptance of one another as partner and in this ritual God is important. This practice is common in most religions. Yet this does not mean that such a marriage is everlasting and that there is no divorce.

Whether Christian, Muslim, Hindu or of any other faith, man is man, and woman is woman. There is nothing spiritual in a marriage today – it is simply a traditional affair, a social convention. The spiritual marriage is a rational, scientific and above all spiritual practice, thus beyond all traditional beliefs. People take the name of God while getting married, they vow fidelity in everything and yet marriages fail. The reason behind it is that they do not know the deep mystical significance of marriage.

Probably the greatest number of rites is performed in the Hindu marriage. There are two types of Hindu marriages, the Vedic and the Puranic. Both are based essentially on the Vedas. However, the Puranic marriage includes a large number of traditional rites and rituals and in general requires more intensive preparation than a Vedic one. Both of them are very beautiful and entertaining.

But the entertainment and joy at a marriage are very shallow and fleeting. And it strips one of a huge amount of money ridiculously spent to please other people. Vedic marriage involves invocation of gods, *panigrahan* (hand grasping), stone stepping and taking vows by walking seven steps with fire as witness (*agnishapath*). The fire ceremony is for the invocation of the gods in whose presence the vows of married life are taken. Married life for the purpose of spiritual evolution is not a simple affair; therefore the blessings of the gods, who are the forces of nature, are important. On our spiritual journey, we will need both material and spiritual wealth. Living in harmony with the forces of nature is therefore essential.

The *panigrahan* or hand grasping ceremony is probably the most important part of the Vedic marriage. Holding the hand of the bride, the bridegroom takes the following vows: "I, the bridegroom hold your hand in mine for prosperity of household life. May you attain old age with pleasure along with me as your husband. God, who is the master of all prosperity, the administrator of justice, creator of the universe and all-subsisting, and the enlightened persons here are giving you to me for the fulfilment of household life's attainments and obligations."

Let us go through the vows one by one. Firstly, the bridegroom says, "I hold your hand in mine for the prosperity of household life." What is prosperity of household life? According to the ancient Indian way of life, marriage is one of the four stages, the other three being celibacy, the life of a hermit and that of a wandering monk. The hermit's life is spent in solitude for intense meditation till God-realization, which is the ultimate possibility of human consciousness. The wandering monk is the symbol of complete freedom from material ties. Spiritual practices that lead to deep meditation need to be started during the student or celibacy stage. During the household stage, another aspect of one's personality unfolds and there is a lot to learn about oneself and the opposite sex, which is conducive towards self-unfolding. Therefore prosperity of household life includes, apart from material progress, spiritual experiments and progress made with the help of the partner. Certain practices of *tantra*, for instance, can be done with the help of an intelligent partner.

Next it says: "May you attain old age with pleasure along with me as your husband." In other words, may we live in a pleasurable manner, without bringing unnecessary suffering into our life. The essence of life is pure joy. Completeness leads to great joy. Each partner being a complement to the other, one feels complete when together, hence the joy is greater. The couple is going to spend a whole life together; therefore if it is not pleasurable then it is not worth staying together. So many people have taken the above oaths while holding each other's hand, yet see how many lives are hellish today, and others continue to get married without any proper understanding of marriage!

The vow further says, "God, who is the master of all prosperity, the administrator of justice, the creator of the universe and all-subsisting, and the enlightened persons here are giving you to me for the fulfilment of household life's attainment and obligations." How many people realize that they are taking the name of God during that sacred ceremony? Are there any enlightened people today in front of whom those ceremonies are performed? Obviously not! If there is an enlightened person anywhere in this world, I am not sure he would like to witness the lies that are being told by both the bride and the bridegroom.

Another important part of the vow is 'the fulfilment of household life's attainment and obligations.' Do these imply material progress and child bearing only? If so, then what is the use of taking God's name and making vows? Many people do it even without taking any vow or getting married. A married life is not fulfilled if one does not realize the divinity within. The names *devi* and *deva* are given respectively to a woman and a man of Hindu faith just to remind them of their divine essence.

The bridegroom continues to take other vows: "I, possessed of virtues and prosperity, grasp your hand, full of inspiration of duty and procreation, and hold your hand into mine. You are my wife in the letter and spirit of dharma and I am your husband accordingly." The first declaration in this vow is, "I, possessed of virtue and prosperity, grasp your hand." How many people, especially those who recite these words during a marriage ceremony, are possessed of virtues? What is a virtue after all? It is the spontaneous behaviour and action of an awakened person. Not of an intellectually awakened person but a spiritually awakened one. Love, for example, is a spontaneous overflow of energy from the soul. Likewise are other virtues like forgiveness, patience and compassion. Today most, I will even say more than 99% of people, are living a life of untruth, fantasy and dreams. How then can they be virtuous? No, I am not talking of bookish or superficial virtue but that which stems from the ocean of the soul. How many can claim through experience that they possess a soul? And in this ritual the bridegroom says, "I, possessed of virtues." Such important vows are taken unconsciously, simply as a formality. This is what makes marriage a social convention.

It further refers to prosperity, that is, "I, with prosperity, grasp your hand." How many bridegrooms can really guarantee a secure material future for themselves and their spouses? Many do not have a house of their own and some do not even have a stable job. I know people who get married with the bare minimum, while others cannot afford even that. Yet, parrot-like, they recite these vows. Another issue is that many do not know Hindi or Sanskrit and very often the priests recite the mantras quickly without caring to explain them. Even if they are explained, the couple do not care at all. What they are waiting for is the end of the ceremony.

The words inspiration, duty and procreation also come under the vow. Both inspiration and duty are almost inexistent today. People do their duty not as duty, that is, not through inspiration and understanding but out of greed, obligation or expectation of reward. Often there is also a spirit of reproach and regret. The bridegroom further says, "I am your husband in the letter and spirit of dharma." 'Letter and spirit of dharma' means in words and according to the laws of nature. The word dharma conceals a meaning that few people understand. I will even say that only enlightened beings understand and can explain its true meaning. The root of the word is *dhri* plus the suffix *man* or *ma* meaning mind. *Dhri* means to hold, to support or to sustain. Therefore dharma is the Mind that sustains everything. Without the Infinite Mind there would be no creation. With It, come the laws that support everything, the particles, their forces, the elements, their characteristics, the planets, galaxies and other moving bodies. All of them are governed by laws and these laws constitute dharma.

Going deeper into dharma is *dharmakaya*, the body of the law, which is nothing but energy. In this vow, dharma refers to the spiritual and material rules that govern the coming and staying together of two opposite forces. There are scientific laws. For example, having a child with a member of one's close relative is unscientific as it can lead to the conception of an unhealthy child. Likes repel. Similarly, the man and the woman should be compatible in many respects, as we have seen earlier.

The third vow pronounced by the bridegroom is the following: "O bride! That you, whom the Protector of the universe gave me, remain supported and nourished by me. O ye procreating lady! May you live hundred autumns delightfully with me as your husband." A worthy partner in all respects is indeed very rare, therefore the bridegroom says, "You whom the Protector of the universe gave me." If she has been given to him by the Lord Himself, then his respect towards the bride must be very great. Also, it implies that the bridegroom has chosen her as bride because of the qualities that God has bestowed on her. Therefore if he has chosen her, it is all by His grace. This is why the groom says, "You are given to me by the Protector of the universe."

This vow ends by the bridegroom's blessings, "May you live, oh procreating lady, hundred autumns delightfully with me as your husband." Everyone has the capacity to bless others and blessing comes from a loving heart and a peaceful mind. The husband here, out of love, blesses his wife to live delightfully. By using the term 'procreating lady,' he gives her the status of a procreative woman.

In the fourth vow the bridegroom says, "O bride! The relation of husband and wife in this world should be in conformity with the teachings of God and the enlightened persons. Just as electricity is permeating all the objects, so you obtain nice dresses, ornaments and happiness from me for the sake of my pleasure. May the all-creating super excellent God bless my wife with offspring! Similarly I will keep you well-dressed and well-ornamented." In the first part of this vow is the statement 'conformity with the teachings of God and the enlightened persons.' First of all, God is not a person having any teachings. Secondly, there are not two separate teachings, that of God and that of the enlightened beings. But I can understand the spirit. 'Teachings of God' means according to the universal laws of truth and these are known to the enlightened beings, who reveal them to the world so that those who are intelligent can put them into practice.

Next we see the importance of dressing beautifully. The husband says, "Let you my wife be beautiful so that I can appreciate and derive pleasure." A woman represents beauty, not as an object but as an aspect of God – she is *sundaram*. A man is the appreciator of that beauty. A person's look is important as a beautiful sight greatly influences the brain. Both husband and wife should be always well-dressed as this has a deep psychological impact. Beauty is an expression of divinity. However, dressing well does not mean spending excessively on fashionable dresses.

In the fifth vow, the bridegroom asks for blessings from the guests attending the wedding ceremony. He says, "O ye our relatives! Kindly be helpful in the well-being of my wife just as the electricity and fire, sun and earth, atmospheric air, oxygen and hydrogen, good fortune, physician and the preacher, impartial ruler, cultured man, Supreme Being, and the moon protect and enhance the lot of subjects and this my wife with prosperity, offspring and so on." Today people go to weddings as a social obligation, to spend time, have good food and for entertainment, and also so that they too may have a certain consideration if ever there is a marriage in their family. They tend to forget the responsibility that it involves.

Nuptial blessing is a great responsibility. Taking part in a marriage means that you are a witness to that marriage and to the vows that the bride and the bridegroom take. If the marriage later fails, one is somehow responsible because one's presence in a wedding indicates that one approves of that union. Here the bridegroom is asking for blessing from the guests, he is requesting them to give as selflessly as the above-mentioned beings, elements, celestial objects and others. How many people can really give such a blessing? Presently, those who get married are blind and are surrounded by blind people like them who know nothing about the truth that a marriage ceremony represents.

We come now to the sixth promise where the bridegroom says, "O bride! Just as I, foreseeing the progress of family through my mind, love your beauty and desire you, so you also be attracted towards me. I leave with good intention thoughts to conceal anything from you and I say, I would not also eat or do anything stealthily. I myself, even not being sturdy, would remove all the obstacles standing in the way of righteousness and you are also expected to act accordingly." So that a married life is successful, it is of paramount importance that there is mutual attraction between husband and wife. This will prove the compatibility between the partners, which is essential for both material and spiritual evolution. Here promise is made to be frank towards each other.

Where there is intimacy and friendship, truth can be easily spoken and listened to, whereas if there is a barrier between husband and wife, union is not possible. The husband says that he will work hard so as to remove all obstacles on the path of righteousness. This means that both husband and wife should tread the path of dharma or righteousness. And let us be very clear, the path of righteousness is quite complex because of the nature of the human mind. It is the path that leads to divinity. The abovementioned oaths are taken by both while the bridegroom is holding the hand of the bride.

These are the six main vows. We are not going into other rites as I consider the above six ones more important since they give an insight into the spiritual dimension of marriage and into life itself. What concerns me is that so many Hindu marriages take place in India, Mauritius and other countries, but almost no one realizes the importance of these vows. People are continuing to take the vows as a mere formality, thus offending a very sacred and even spiritual ceremony.

A very popular tradition related to the Hindu marriage is the *haldi* ceremony. There is great insistence on this ceremony despite the fact that many people do not know its origin and the reason behind it. *Haldi* means turmeric. Both the bride and the groom are almost bathed with turmeric paste. This is accompanied by a ritual after which kith and kin take pleasure in rubbing the paste on different parts of the body of the future bride or groom. The truth behind this ceremony is that turmeric has the property of cleansing the skin and making it fresh and smooth. The future bride and the bridegroom are supposed to rub this paste over their body for about one week prior to the marriage ceremony so that they appear more beautiful. More importance is given to the face, as people's attention is more drawn to that part of the body when it is a question of beauty.

Nowadays the younger generation has started overlooking the *haldi* ceremony and a few others. There is nothing religious or spiritual to it and it can be skipped or performed, it all depends on the individual. It can be said to be esthetical rather than religious.

The rites related to a Christian marriage appear to be very simple. The bride and bridegroom have to give their consent to their marriage in front of the priest and guests. The priest approves the union, telling the couple that they are supposed to be together for better and for worse, whatever are the circumstances, till they are separated by death. The bride and the bridegroom exchange rings. This is followed by a discourse by the priest on the sacredness of marriage and the way a married couple should live. In the Bible, it is written that whatever God has united should not be separated. It seems that people do not heed the words from the Bible as there are so many divorces. The most remarkable thing here is that a priest is a celibate and a theologian, not an enlightened being. Does he know anything about the mystical dimension of men and women to perform a marriage?

In the Christian marriage also, it is a question of promising to sacrifice everything to support each other in difficult circumstances. In front of the guests, two persons accept to be united in body, mind, heart and soul till death separates them, yet many such couples divorce so easily without bearing in mind that they had once made a promise. The people who attend the ceremony are supposed to be witnesses to a sacred union. Still, they do not feel concerned about the fact that the husband and wife owe them certain explanations regarding a divorce. In a church the guests are invited as participants to give blessings and to bear witness to the union. Do they not have any responsibility vis-à-vis the couple? Likewise, does the couple not have any responsibility towards those who were there as witnesses?

Life is simple but it is we people who complicate matters. Few or none know the responsibility of being a witness to a marriage, be it a civil or a religious one. Just like those who stand as witnesses for a civil marriage assume full responsibility for testifying to the marriage and also that the bride and the bridegroom are not already married, the guests at a religious marriage too should bear their responsibilities.

The Family

In common parlance, a family is a unit comprised of a husband, a wife and child or children. In some families, there are also grandparents and even in-laws. Families that share the same surname are close relatives, then come relatives by union. If we go to the root of the family tree, we will see that we are all members of a large family. And these days it is very much a question of the slogan, 'The world is a whole family.' However, being a member of a family does not mean much today. It certainly does not make one a better individual. There are innumerable families that are broken due to disagreements on property and wealth or other problems.

Life is a big university. Every stage has its own lessons that we have to learn so as to attain the ultimate aim of life. In a family, there is so much to learn and to share. People do not come together by mere coincidence. Each member of a family must have had a relationship with one another in a previous incarnation or if it is the first time, they surely have to learn from or to teach others. However, learning and sharing become possible only when there is freedom, detachment, attentiveness and most important of all, inner silence.

The way family units evolve today does not reflect the above virtues. The root cause of this absence is possessiveness, attachment, excessive emotion and the arrogance of being a parent. On one hand, parents tend to forget that they are merely 'doors' and that children are not their possessions but their responsibilities. Children are human beings formed by the Supreme Will in the womb. Therefore mothers should be grateful towards existence instead of becoming possessive, as is the case generally. The attitude of taking their children as objects, on which they have every right and expectation, has destroyed the very possibility of motherhood, which is most important for the physical, mental, emotional and spiritual growth of a child.

Possessiveness, attachment and emotion form a very thick veil that prevents one from seeing the truth of life. A plant that is exposed to too much sunlight will get burnt and growth will stop. Equally, if it is over-exposed to wind or over-watered, it will die. If it is left on its own and not taken care of, it can become infected with diseases and become barren. Similarly, children should be cared for by giving them the right amount of affection, love, education and seriousness, without being carried away by emotion. This is very rare and parents refuse to acknowledge that either they have pampered their children or they have failed to provide them with the best education (not solely academic), which is the reason why the children grow in the wrong manner and thus they fail to learn the lessons of life.

Like a seed, a family too has to expand. This does not imply that there is a need to have many individuals in a family. But it certainly means that parents should not bind children to them. They should rather help their children to go out in life and explore it. I know many parents who will not accept that their children go abroad for learning or live separately after marriage. There is also the reality that daughters-in-law and mothers-in-law are in a state of perpetual conflict. In the few cases of apparently good relations, compromise and hypocrisy are prevalent.

If the children have been given the right education, then why fear all these things? Family life is also like a temple. We do not stay there forever; instead we learn from it and then go further to experiment what we have learned. This does not necessarily mean leaving the house of one's parents, though many times it becomes inevitable. But it certainly means detachment to allow mental and emotional growth. We are all individuals, but so long as we do not get detached from one another, there is no possibility of realizing our individuality. And when there is no individuality, how can we become the cosmic person, which is the ultimate aim of human existence?

Many times it happens that, due to poor economic conditions, there is no choice but to live under the same roof, then the situation becomes very difficult unless there is great understanding and the couples manage to live in freedom. Otherwise, things can be very chaotic. My advice is that one should be financially stable before entering married life. Know that marriage is not an obligation but a choice. Parents should understand that their children have their own individuality and are not their possession on which they can exercise rights as they wish.

Even today, many families are deeply attached to the traditional way of living, especially among Asians. In such a milieu, the father or at times the mother is the boss, and the parents are given the status of gods. They have an overall hand over the family business and their say predominates in many matters, even in the choice of spouses for their children. These people have not grown and their children have retained the mindset of old people. Therefore, they reason likewise and remain mostly traditional. Many people refuse to tread the spiritual path because they take their parents as their gods. The future of such people will always remain a potential, without the possibility of being actualized. They are like bonsai as they have been emotionally blackmailed, either directly or indirectly.

The whole attitude of people regarding marriage, relationship and family life should change. The Asian concept of extended family is the cause of many conflicts. In ancient times, it was convenient but now we are in a different era. The seed has to break so that it can become a tree. The branches of a tree are at times very distant, yet they are one with the tree and they do not possess or hinder each other's growth. Families should learn from that. Though being relatives or close ones, we can live separately and be on good terms.

"My family is my everything," many people say. Why is man's or woman's life limited to his or her family? Life is so vast. There are so many things that stand to be discovered and experienced which are so beautiful, peace-giving, blissful and liberating, yet people are tied up to their own petty world. Man is so unconscious that his vision does not go beyond his senses. Whatever he has achieved today is based on his empirical knowledge. But how vast is the world beyond! If only man and woman could understand each other, a door to the beyond would open.

It needs individuals to make a family. From families a society is born and from society a nation. Thus a nation is a big family and it becomes prosperous and powerful when all families in it are happy and peaceful. But a family can only be happy and peaceful when each of its members is intelligent and loving. These two virtues are proper to each individual, but presently they are buried deep within us.

The purpose of education is to bring them up. However, we see that knowledge, pedagogy and education as a whole have failed in this endeavour. No wonder it has not succeeded in bringing people to realize that love, peace, harmony and intelligence constitute the very soul of a civilized society. Instead of focusing on the individual, it has focused on the superfluous needs of people by spending great amount of time and energy on the means that could provide the superfluous needs.

Still, man has not become more joyful, peaceful and loving. It is the contrary that has become true. We live in a society that calls itself civilized, yet almost everyone is ignorant about the deepest truth reflecting his self.

The Beauty and Secret of Family Life

Family life is not a random stroke of evolution. It is a very deep strategy or plan brought by the force of evolution for our higher growth. However, due to our ignorance, we do not know how to benefit from it. And as with everything else bestowed upon us, we have turned it into a curse instead of using it as a blessing.

It is indeed very difficult to tread the journey of life all alone, without any close company. But in one sense, when one bears in mind the innumerable difficulties one can face with the other, it is better to do it alone rather than have a partner. Life adventure with a partner or with a group of persons in the form of a family can be beautiful and beneficial only to intelligent people. However, when we see how family or couple life fails lamentably, we cannot but ask, "Does this mean that all those people are unintelligent?" They are intelligent, but just enough to live the way they are. If people were really intelligent, then the world would be a paradise today and few would bother to know whether there is a paradise in some corner of space.

Life is an adventure that should normally be undertaken in group for various reasons. Imagine a man or a woman alone going on an adventure. This has its own beauty, nevertheless it lacks something. Fun will be missing. The adventure of life should not be like crossing a desert, dry and monotonous, though passing through a desert for a while has its own excitement. It should be like going into the woods with flowers, animals, waterfalls, mountains and singing birds, enjoying rain, clouds, sun and the blue sky. Family life should be with smile, laughter, tears, playfulness, challenges, temptations, doubts, separation, sharing and so on and so forth.

A family should consist of souls who are willing to evolve, not people who want to stagnate and compromise with the vicious circle of the senses, mind and emotions. For this reason, a family should be wisely constructed. Now, this may seem strange though we often use the term. We do construct a family, but it always fails to bring about the true result.

How to build a family based on love and wisdom? The most important element is understanding, without which nothing good is achieved. But what should we understand first of all? The purpose or the ultimate possibility of human existence. Due to the absence of this first and foremost truth of life, humanity has gone astray. Once we achieve the right understanding, a great revolution will take place and the whole of mankind will change direction. Presently, we are sidetracked.

The ultimate possibility of human consciousness is cosmic in nature. In other words, man's consciousness is presently like a seed that can be sown and made to germinate, grow, flower and bear fruits. Planting the seed of human consciousness and helping it to grow and blossom is what I call the art and science of religion or the mystical science. Therefore, we find that nothing can be dissociated from religion. Of course, I am talking of religion in its purest state and here I would prefer to call it meditation. Love, willpower, intuition, virtue, inner peace, all these come through meditation and family life can greatly help in bringing in meditation. How?

As I have said, it is not easy to tread the journey of life all by oneself, though there have been a few cases. When several intelligent people come together, the result is greater intelligence and thus greater creativity. If the right partner is chosen, then it is possible to call and give birth to highly evolved souls. And with the coming of highly evolved souls, the family unit becomes powerful, loving, creative and vibrant. In such an atmosphere the lessons of life can be easily learnt. On the way to explore one's ultimate possibility, there are many challenges. In a family, one can be encouraged and helped as the other members are on the same path.

When intelligent and loving people come together, a house becomes a temple of wisdom and devotion, thus ushering one further towards cosmic consciousness instead of towards attachment, quarrel, jealousy and indifference. Human relationship is a very beautiful phenomenon, but only when there is no attachment because it blurs the mind. When this happens, reality is veiled and may even appear as unreality. One may also see unreality as reality. Much delusion is created through attachment and excessive emotion. It is nearly impossible to stick to truth when attachment has gripped the mind and emotion has overpowered the heart.

Mutual understanding, supporting and correcting one another and sticking to truth, however bitter it may be, are the most important challenges in family life. Members of a family should not camouflage untruth or the fault of one another as this will be like nurturing a deadly cobra, which will sooner or later spread its poison. Each person in a family has to understand that everyone is an individual and should be free in body, mind and heart. There should be no emotional blackmailing. If any member of a family wishes to move away, he should be helped and supported. We should not forget that as the tree grows, its branches and leaves, which were in a potential state, move apart – this is called growth.

No one should possess or try to possess anybody, for it is the worst kind of violence. We are all souls on a journey, we have to learn, grow and evolve and this is very much a personal affair. Others can only help. They should not be a hindrance on the way. A family where such wisdom shines becomes a temple indeed and a buddha-field is created there. This can be further strengthened by the practice of group meditation. A house where there is not at least one hour of meditation and devotional practice is not worthy of being called a house. Devotional practice does not mean the mere repetition of old age beliefs or borrowed words that one recites parrot-like for a few minutes. It is the sincere and intense love for God and the means that can inflame it. Singing His praise with the accompaniment of good music, study of scriptures and worship create a divine atmosphere in the house.

Today married life is based on possessiveness and each one thinks the other is mine therefore I have every right on him or her. It is strange that in our so-called civilized society, there is rape even in married life and some cases are reported to the police. This throws light into the kind of environment in which children evolve. Many houses have a very impure atmosphere indeed. "I am for no one, no one belongs to me," this should be a mantra and realising it will liberate one from possessiveness, which is the greatest weakness in human relationship. Many errors and much suffering happen because of it.

While a house should be a temple and each member a potential god, it is sad to note that many houses are the habitats of evil. Members of a family come together due to some karmic forces. As such, they share something in common. Understanding this can help to solve many problems and also in the evolution of the mind and the heart. The basic lesson, however, is to be ready to learn and for this the mind and the body have to be prepared. Bearing all this in mind, the house can be said to be a school where much can be gained indeed. If parents are compatible individuals, the children too will have a high degree of compatibility and this favours learning. Of course, there are exceptions. In other words, most members of a family may be compatible save one who does not fit in. That too has its own importance and there is certainly a lesson to draw from it.

Therefore we see that a house is not a mere building for shelter and a family is not the mere congregation of people bound through attachment, emotion or duty. Members of a sane family are like parts that form a whole. If the parts have the required characteristics, then a whole is formed and such a whole is very powerful, especially if each one is trained in the spiritual science. A sane family has a special characteristic and place in the universe. It is like an antenna that can attract much good, both material and spiritual.

Look at a picture of Shiv Parivar, the divine family. Though Shiva and Satti are opposites, they complement each other and live in such harmony. In fact, opposites are meant to complement each other, not to fight with one another. Do not matter and energy, darkness and light, good and bad, hot and cold, fire and water cohabit or coexist in the same universe? It is strange how everything, even Satan, has a place in this universe! How is all this possible? They all live in harmony and according to their own nature. Man is a replica of the universe in miniature for God created us according to His own image and likeness, as says the Bible. Therefore all the opposite but complementary forces must exist in us too. Then how is it that man and woman cannot live in harmony as the Shiv Parivar?

The Shiv Parivar symbolises the substratum of existence, the eternal couple of consciousness and energy, and the various forces that come into existence as a result of their union. The two sons, Ganesha and Muruga, and the host of animals symbolize the dual and multiple forces that live in harmony. Try to imagine a serpent by the side of a mouse, or a peacock on a snake, or still a bull and a lion in the same harem.

An ideal married life should be a Shiv Parivar, but this is not easily achieved - one has to strive for it. It is a unit symbolizing an ideal family and since the family is the basic unit of a society, the whole of human society can become a peaceful, loving, creative and harmonious garden where all can enjoy life.

The Fallacy of Marriage Today

Can we imagine how life would be if there were no marriage? Imagine a world without a family unit! There are many people, especially in European countries, who live together and have children without entering wedlock. Does this mean that they are less good than those who have gone through the rites of a wedding? To love, do we need to perform a ritual? Today the rites of a religious marriage are as mechanical and formal as the formalities of a civil marriage, which prove that there is no love and trust. The performance of religious marriages is actually a blind adherence to age-old traditions.

Can two persons not simply love and live together without any bondage? What is a wedding ceremony or a civil marriage today if not a bondage and an attachment? Once the deed is signed or the wedding is over, one becomes as if the owner of the other. Yes, two partners can become good co-travellers or friends, but not the possession of each other.

Like religious ceremonies, marriage too is nowadays based on superficiality and glamour. People do everything save the real marriage, which is something spiritual, thus pure and sublime. A marriage ceremony today is just another opportunity to gratify the senses, display one's arrogance and fulfil desires. Most weddings take place with great pomp and celebration. The preparations can last for several months. Much money is spent and most of the time it is to please other people, not necessarily the bride and the bridegroom.

Some persons skip the conventional style of marriage and choose to simply co-habit with a partner to avoid the high cost involved in a marriage ceremony. There is a case about a girl who had opted to forgo the traditional marriage ceremony and who had in return asked her parents to give her the amount they intended to spend so that she could make judicious use of it. Unfortunately, her parents were narrow-minded and conditioned people who insisted for a religious marriage at any cost. The result was that she chose to cohabit with the man of her choice without marriage rites.

It is a big contradiction that while huge amounts of money are spent in a wedding, after some years, again much money is spent to fight the case for a divorce. The partners, who only a few years back were irresistibly drawn towards each other, are now at daggers drawn. A marriage ceremony is also an occasion to boost up one's ego. It is a question of honour and dignity in society, despite tensions resulting from impositions or disagreements. For example, there are young lovers who start to quarrel before marriage, but are unable to break apart for some reason. What is stupid and amusing at the same time is that some people divorce to remarry with the same pomp and celebration. In some cases, this may happen several times. Of course, with each partner, one will take the same oath and perform the same rituals, again taking the name of God and so on.

Another amusing fact is that everyone wants to have the most good-looking and chaste partner. Few will care to look at themselves in a mirror and raise questions about their own chastity. Here I wish to retell a story that Osho narrated to his disciples. Once, a young man went in search of a bride. He reached a matrimonial agency where a signpost said: "Choose your best partner." With much excitement the fellow stepped in the agency. At the entrance were two doors; on the first one was written 'Beautiful Girl' and on the other 'Ordinary Girl.' Obviously, our friend opened the first door. Therein he saw two more doors with the inscriptions 'Virgin' and 'Non-virgin' respectively. Without hesitation, he proceeded to the 'Virgin' door. Again he came across two doors where he had to choose between 'Rich Partner' and 'Poor Partner'. Of course, he chose the 'Rich Partner' door. Then he had to select between 'Intelligent Girl' and 'Ordinary Girl.' Who would not choose an intelligent girl! When he opened the door, he saw a note written in bold characters: "Now look at your face in the mirror!"

People want to have the best partner without themselves possessing the best qualities that they seek in others. Almost everyone is disillusioned after marriage when one realizes that actual life is very different from what one fancied. In the world of thought, one can dream of a perfect partner, but reality is altogether different. Nature is not here to fulfil our dreams. On the contrary, she is always finding ways and means to break our slumber. But it is so deep that though we are shaken every time, still we continue to hope for a better tomorrow. And when tomorrow proves again to be disastrous, we are frustrated and at times even ruined.

On many wedding cards, it is written: "Marriages are arranged in heaven and celebrated on earth." In others, a mantra is inscribed at the top. I wonder what people understand by a marriage 'arranged in heaven.' Do they mean that the partners were chosen by God? If this were true, then a lot of questions could be raised. The first one is, how come that something divinely arranged goes so wrong and even ends in a divorce? Should God bother to choose our partner? Then what are we here for? If we look around, it does not seem that God chooses our partner. For if He did so, then all couples would be perfectly happy together. Is it the case?

We should start thinking about ourselves seriously because things have always fallen apart so far as marriage is concerned. If marriage is arranged above, then here on earth, it should be a constant celebration. Is it? It is not, it is rather a problem. We overlook its sacredness and instead focus on its material side. For many people married life is a hell. How can it start in heaven and end in hell? The cause is surely within us. Why do we not seek it within? Who cares to know all this? We are here simply to blindly follow society, tradition, instinct and our distorted reasoning.

Today marriage is like an imprisonment where you have to live according to certain norms and rules. A wife smiling to another man or saying, "How handsome and brave he is!" is considered as committing a great offence to the husband. Likewise, a man should better not praise another woman for her intelligence and beauty in front of his wife. Neither the man nor the woman has the right to commit the least mistake. If, for instance, a partner commits adultery, the other feels terribly aggrieved as if something extremely precious has been taken away from him or her. The reason for such a reaction is not that they are themselves saints, but because their ego is badly shaken. Their partner going out with another one conveys a few bitter messages to them. It may mean that the other is better in some ways; he or she may be richer, more beautiful, more intelligent, more sensual and so on.

Let me be very clear: I support neither male nor female infidelity. I am simply reporting facts. It is a scientific fact that man is polygamous by nature. And I am always in favour of transcending human nature. My point here is that a partner who feels betrayed personalizes the matter and completely forgets natural human traits. The emotional and even mental reactions often lead to physical violence. One may find something wrong without being drowned by it. However, when one is possessive or deeply attached to a person, a thing or a principle, then one can be greatly disturbed. The ego gets a great blow because of its identification to the particular person, thing or principle. Is it not possible to discuss the matter with understanding, help the person, consider his situation and then decide what course of action to take? Why should one get carried away by anger, hatred and jealousy and do unwanted things?

The Great Illusion

A very common feature today in all weddings is that the events are recorded on video and kept as a souvenir. I have watched a few such films. In one of them, a discourse was given by one of the guests. Glass in hand, he was praising the parents of the newly married couple and then said, "This is real love between two young persons, which they have decided to culminate into marriage." Hearing this, I told those who were watching the film together with me that this is the type of love that ends up in court. And the same fellow who made this discourse would then try to justify the lawsuit and be on the side of the party related to him. It seemed that the person, though he was quite old, had not known life. Despite the fact that he must have known that many such marriages are unsuccessful, he brought the word 'love' in his discourse. What do these people know about love? Instead he could have said, "I hope that you learn to love or to understand each other."

Man keeps on doing the same mistake again and again; he does not learn his lesson. It is like in the Mahabharata where one brother went to fetch water in a nearby lake. As he was about to quench his thirst, he heard a voice asking him not to drink water from the lake and warning him that if he did so, he would die. But overpowered by thirst, he did not heed the command and consequently died. The other three brothers met with the same fate. The fifth one, who was wiser, listened to the voice and reflected upon the situation. He was not overpowered by his thirst. He then realized that he was being tested for his wisdom. When he satisfied the supernatural force guarding the lake, his brothers were brought back to life.

This is a very significant story. Man is obsessed by worldly pleasures. He does not discriminate, thus is carried away and dies. The man of wisdom has mastered his desires and therefore he is able to save his physical, emotional, mental and spiritual qualities represented by the four brothers. Similarly, people who get married do not know the reality about marriage; they are in the grips of lust, conditionings, tradition and desire. Only the wise takes the right decision, but then a wise is absolutely rare these days. It seems as if people contract a marriage so as to appear normal, even if the marriage will break sooner or later. Human nature is such that a person is carried away by his ignorance to such an extent that he keeps on making mistakes, and when he is faced with himself, he denies it and tries to justify his action.

Here I wish to make a small digression. During the Deepavali festival, people clean the house, prepare cakes, wear beautiful clothes, light lamps and enjoy themselves. Many people give much importance to decorating their house and for some it is even a question of prestige to have the best decoration. On that day we share cakes with neighbours and relatives. But where is Deepavali in all that? How easily is it said that Deepavali is symbolical of the victory of light upon darkness! How many people have realized this? How many have vanquished evil or darkness? People do not realize that where there is light, there is no darkness, so the question of victory does not pose. Where there is Godliness, there is no evil. These are related to Deepavali, nevertheless the digression is pertinent as marriage too has become like this. We do everything save the marriage of the souls. It is easily said that marriage is the meeting of two souls, yet people are very far away from that sublime realization. People do not know whether they have a soul, what is a soul, yet they talk of the union of souls.

Souls meet where there is love, harmony and peace. This happens after much study, spiritual practice and after going through many ups and downs in life. How can souls meet when there is jealousy, possessiveness, I and you? How can souls meet when one is still a body and all relationships start and end with the body? People take the intensity of emotional attachment to be love. How wrong they are! Love is a silent yet infinitely vibrating presence that does not start and end with the body. It is no doubt present in the body but also pervades every particle of existence. How can it then be limited to one person? It is all-encompassing. Love is not blind because it is conscious and omnipresent.

A large number of people take their partner to be life's be-all and end-all. The balance is heavier on the wife's side because for her the husband is everything. Some women say, "My husband is my god, my family is my worship and everything else." I wonder how the world would be if this were true.

Women often say, "I prefer to have a husband who stays loyal to me than have all the material comfort and things in life." In other words, a loyal husband is all that most women want and they can sacrifice anything for this. From this, one might believe that they really love their husband. But the reality is quite different, though it is true that a woman's life revolves around the man of her life. It is only recently that women have started to expand their horizon beyond their traditional world. The deeper reality is that when a man chooses a woman as his partner, whether it is for marriage or for flirting, the woman understands, "I am being chosen among others, therefore I am worth something." Disloyalty means to her that she is not as good as the other woman or is even inferior. And this is unbearable for her. Another fact is that when a woman finds a man who has some compatibility with her, then he becomes part of her life. Therefore adultery would mean that a part of her is being snatched away and here also the pain becomes unbearable.

Man has a different trouble. When a woman is drawn towards another man instead of him or if the wife or the beloved is disloyal to him, his ego gets a big blow. He feels that his masculinity is at stake and is being challenged. A man can tell a thousand and one lies to draw and keep a woman to him. Few people realize that the attraction between the opposite sexes is based on many factors. These are physical, instinctual, emotional, mental, psychical and even spiritual attractions.

I recall having said, in a spiritual gathering, that our real partner is God and that real marriage is between Him and us. One person then told me, "But what will happen to the world if we all marry God and remain celibate?" In reply, I first asked the person, "What progress has man made by having a human partner and where has marriage led us?" Secondly, I asked him, "Why should we think in the place of God?" Let Him manage His own business. He should know what to do, for He knows fairly well that we can always choose to remain celibate. Finally, I told the person that I have never been against marriage, I myself being a married man. However, we should consider our human partner as a friend, a co-traveller and an aid in our spiritual practice. It should not be like buying a slave or keeping a servant. Our partner should not be an object to be possessed nor should we be blindly attached to him or her as is the case today.

Most people want their partner to be like them. They do not realize the uniqueness of each individual and this state of affairs gives rise to a lot of conflict. If everybody becomes alike, then uniqueness will be lost. The human drama will not only become ugly but may brutally come to an end due to a very chaotic situation. Diversity of character without stooping to a base behaviour is important, not similarity of character. But it is true that when there is too much difference between partners, cohabitation becomes very difficult or even unbearable. In this context, the partners must sort out the problem before coming together.

Unfortunately, people do not think well before deciding to live together. After all, few people show their real face before marriage. Most of them are masked, hiding their ugly face behind a façade. Besides, most individuals are not aware of certain aspects of their own behaviour until they start living with someone else. Life is a great adventure. Before deciding to live permanently with a partner, one must reflect deeply and my understanding is that mere thinking will not do. An insight into the general character of the future partner must be acquired by means of the sciences of astrology, numerology, palmistry, auras and others. As explained earlier, through these, one can have an idea of the character of the person with whom one is planning to embark on the adventure of married life.

One may live a whole life with a partner without knowing the depth of his or her mind. Sometimes, totally unexpected things turn up and that too after many years of cohabitation. For example, a wife may sadly realize after many years of marriage that her husband is a homosexual or a paedophile. A man may find that his wife has eloped with another person or is having an affair. People will say that they never imagined such a thing could happen after so many years together.

Many couples are carrying on because of their children, parents or society. A compromise is made, which they call a sacrifice. Perhaps it is a sacrifice in some sense, accepting to undergo the hellish conditions for the sake of children. Such a compromise is not always good because of the tense atmosphere it creates at home. Others play their roles by giving the impression that everything is going on smoothly and that they are ideal partners, though there is great hypocrisy deep within.

Separation or Divorce

I recall having attended the eve of a marriage ceremony of someone who happened to be a spiritual seeker. After having dinner with friends and disciples, I went to meet the future bridegroom. At that moment he was going to light a lamp, which according to rituals is lit by the bridegroom on the eve of his marriage as worship to God. When the lamp was lit, I told the young man, "One thing has to be remembered. Today you have lit this lamp, henceforth it will require much sacrifice, understanding, sharing and love from both you and your wife to keep it burning." I was referring to a successful married life. What I learned afterwards did not shock me much because I know that such possibilities always exist. After the honeymoon, the marriage was broken for apparently no solid reason. Then I reminded the disciples who had attended the ceremony of the pomp and display we had witnessed at the wedding of that person. How easily a marriage is broken! Where is its sacredness?

During courtship if we observe the young lovers and future couples, we will not have the least idea that one day they will be at daggers drawn and will end up in a law court, with a sharp competitive mind as to who will have the larger share of wealth and who will have the custody of the child or children, as the case may be. Yet these things happen all too often. There are so many people who are living under the same roof, but they are as if already divorced. In the case of a divorce, it is the children who become the greatest victims as the adults are able to manage anyhow.

Divorce means separation, but allow me to ask some simple questions. Was there any union in the first place that we now speak of divorce? Do physical bodies really meet? When we say that the hearts meet, are we referring to the blood-pumping device? How do feelings meet? My own observation is that marriages fail and will continue to fail because people do not know what it is and why they marry. Therefore, the result is bound to be as it is at present and I maintain that divorce will not stop.

Marriages will be mechanical so long as we do not realise that we are in reality much more than a body. We are a soul and our being has different layers. Man and woman, though they have the same potentialities, are quite different. Till now very few people, not even 0.5%, have known and understood that man and woman are different and thus their behaviours are bound to be different in many respects. It is as if men are from Mars and women from Venus. Although we have seven layers, each one related to and superimposed on one another, we are living and behaving as if we had only one layer – the physical one. The consequence is chaotic. Until and unless we go deep into our differences and see how we can come together in spite of the superficial nature of our qualities, I see no bright future both for marriage and for the earth itself.

Marriage is the birth of a family and a family is the base for children who are the leaders of tomorrow. Judge for yourself, dear readers, what kind of society we will have if the very base where future leaders are born, is itself uncertain and polluted! From the book of John Gray 'Men are from Mars and Women from Venus', we get an insight into one of the reasons why things may start falling apart quite foolishly in a married life. Gray says that we mistakenly assume that if our partners love us, they will react and behave in a certain way. The way we react and behave when we love someone is very crucial.

Man is an aggressive force while the woman is a passive one but vibrant with feelings. There is a big difference in our metabolism. When women are having their menses, they react differently to certain things and their moods are different. It is all a question of hormonal release. Gray also says that the most frequently expressed complaint of women against men is that men do not listen. When she speaks to him, he either ignores her or gives her a solution to quickly get over with her. Few men realise that a woman likes to be listened to with care and attention first, then if the need be, she will ask for a solution. Men do not have much patience to listen and women like to go into every detail.

One of the causes of feminine adultery is that a woman feels very good when she meets someone who is ready to listen to her with patience and cares for her. Of course, when a man wants to have a woman, he will develop the patience of listening to anything, though when his wife speaks he will pray when she will end her discourse! On the other hand, a man's virility is perceived through his ability to achieve results. Therefore to offer a man an unsolicited advice is to presume that he does not know what to do or that he cannot do it. Instead of encouraging him, the wife will say, "Call Mr. so and so, he is used to it ..." and this displeases the man. In such a case, the woman should be tactful and encourage him with words like: "You have the ability to do it, I am sure you will succeed. I am with you." Then things could take a different turn.

However, there are many other big differences that we have to know and understand. Also, we should realise that we have the ability to go beyond what nature has given us. For example, a man must realise that when his wife is saying, "You will not be able to do it, call someone else," she may be right. If this is the case, then he must develop the courage to face the truth and therein is his real manliness. It is absolutely important to know that we have a brain, which is divided into two main parts and other sub-parts, and that these do not operate in the same way in both sexes.

Both are physically different, have a different family background, are more than ninety percent unconscious and no matter how long these two persons have stayed together, whatever one knows of the other represents only approximately one percent of his or her character. This is a well-known psychological fact. Partners always believe that things will be fine. Even after having known how previous couples have behaved, they escape the fact that things may go wrong with them too. No one is ever ready to believe that they are not dealing with saints and that human beings err. People are not prepared to expect the worst, instead they are always hoping for the best.

There are innumerable cases where people compromise and are caught in a powerful chain of obligations. When people have a certain amount of intelligence, fruitful discussion is possible. But what if it is absent? Then life becomes hellish. The issue of divorce is not new and has existed since ancient times as all other problems created by man. Yet people are still being strongly carried away by it. And we claim to be living in a civilised world! Divorce should be the last resort, when it is found that there is absolutely no other way to settle matters.

It is said that future couples should be educated as to the realities of married life. But who will do that? The possibility of divorce is concealed in one and all because people are not yet enlightened and therefore are ignorant about their own nature. Furthermore, those who pretend to know or teach about married life are not aware of the truth that human life neither starts with the body nor ends with it. Only a mystic can give the advice. But a mystic is absolutely rare. There have been so many fakes around, so how to recognise one? Most people think they know and are not ready to stoop to learn. It requires a certain degree of intelligence to realise that this illness and all others originate from ignorance of the truth concerning oneself and one's psychic layers.

Let people understand the difference among the following: lust, passion, desire, emotional attraction, physical attraction, cunningness, fear and love. Apart from love, all the others are from the ego. They have nothing to do with love. Lust is physical attraction and desire; passion is lust with feelings. Desire springs from lust. One may desire someone without any love or intention to marry. Passion may lead to marriage but this does not last long. Cunningness too may lead to marriage because here the person is always mathematical and calculating the profits and other advantages of getting married with a well-to-do partner or someone who has a high social status. Since their relationship is based mainly on certain characteristics, some people seek justification for divorce so that another partner can be conquered. People justify coming together because of their so-called love, again they justify getting married, and finally they justify splitting.

People are very possessive and jealous. Marriage today is like a business. The marriage contract is like a business contract. In most cases the man has the sole and ultimate say in most matters. This macho attitude is far stronger when the woman does not have any academic background and does not work. Women should not be too dependent on their husbands because this can be a great problem in case of a split where the woman will have to struggle to stand on her own feet.

When one goes into the causes of a separation, it becomes obvious that people do not grow beyond the first two layers (physical and emotional). Many times couples behave like stubborn children. One should be ripe for marriage not only physically but also emotionally and mentally. Otherwise married life is bound to fail. Premature marriages should be discouraged as there is a time for everything.

In ancient India, boys and girls went to a sort of university called *gurukul* where they were prepared to face life. Today such an institution is absent. People are now made to be machines that can survive and reproduce. And when they are faced with the harsh realities of life, they are badly shaken. Marriage should be based on love but also on mutual understanding and agreement. Divorce too should be a mutual agreement. Why should one part with hatred and much sadness in one's heart?

Who would believe that many marriages fail because the partners are not satisfied with their sex life, often due to poor communication? There is a strong hesitation on their part to express themselves freely on the subject. It is strange that though partners do not dare to do or talk about certain things with each other, they do not hesitate to talk about them with others. Therefore, I maintain that poor sexual education and making sex a taboo are the causes of failure of many marriages.

One of the many reasons for a split is the question of equality. If man and woman were equal, then there would have been no point in having both genders. One does not require much intelligence to recognize that the difference is vast. Both are God's creatures and have the same potentiality, nevertheless one is more apt to do certain things than the other. Men have exploited women too much in the past and even today this ugly situation persists. Now when women are revolting and paving their way for a better position and proclaiming their real status and nature, the ego of men is hurt and this leads to a split because men always had the lead and now he finds himself in difficulty. A few women are also going against their nature.

Most people believe that they are infallible, though they will say, "We all do err." To err is human and those who err have to be forgiven to some extent. However, this does not mean that beyond a certain limit, one acquires the right to punish those who err. When a person repeats the same error, it means that he is not learning his lesson and is not making any progress. Many times, a split can be avoided by forgiveness, but this virtue is absolutely rare. Those who get married are supposed to be mature and thus grown up, yet such is not the case.

Parents and Conjugal Problems

Parents are possessive, blinded by attachment and have the tendency to interfere in the affairs of their married children and most of the time this ends in a broken marriage. Some parents do not investigate carefully into matters leading their children to court for a divorce. They always tend to side with their children, even if the latter are wrong. Also, some parents get their children married only for the sake of marriage to conform to social norms. Whether there will be a divorce afterwards, nobody cares.

Parents should not take everything that their children say about their conjugal life for granted. They should advise their children with discrimination and without being carried away by feelings. Everything should be done to save a marriage that is worth saving. Parents should not seek to influence or impose their views on their children while advising. They must be bold enough to admit their ignorance on certain matters. Today it is very difficult to have parents who know what truly a marriage is and why they themselves got married. Many children have grown up in an atmosphere of a failing marriage. Then who would advise them?

There are also cases where parents need to give full support to their married children, otherwise their life may be ruined. Many, who are rejected by both partner and parents, tend to commit suicide. Once the children are married, parents should not think that their duties towards them are over. However, this does not imply that they have to interfere into the private life of a couple. It is the duty of every parent to see that after marriage their children are living well because as elders, they are supposed to be wiser, though wisdom does not come with age but with experience and awareness. In any case, there should not be much interference on the part of the parents. Also, married persons should pay heed to elders' advice, instead of following them blindly.

Those who conceive do not know the amount of responsibility they are putting on themselves. If people reflect deeply on that and the quality of life they will have to give to their children, then I am not sure that many would like to become parents. But people are attracted and carried away by the feeling and pleasure of having a child. This veils their minds to such an extent that they have no time to think of its future.

Parents should understand that their children are not their better half and that their children are not theirs. A child is a soul that has assumed a body and right now is still young. He has come here for a special training to realise his soul and parents are no more than mediums. However, since they have invited that particular soul, they have high responsibility towards him. Their responsibility is to help that particular soul to have a solid material, emotional and intellectual foundation to enable it to go through the process of the ultimate alchemy of life, that is, its union with the Supreme Soul. It is quite understandable that parents will find it hard to digest this. But this is the ultimate truth concerning the relationship of parents to their children.

Most people are not aware of or are not ready to acknowledge the fact that though we have come from our parents, we have to be more intimate to our partner than to them. The partner is the one who will help us to awaken our divinity. He/she is the better half, not the father or the mother. It is not that once we embrace married life, we have no more to do with our parents. I am simply stating that our life partner is henceforth the wife or the husband. Therefore, everything should be done to nurture a strong relationship between husband and wife.

Today, many parents influence their children as to the way they should lead their married life. Much attachment of the partners to their respective parents creates marital instability, as there is a tendency to give more importance to parents than to the partner. There is also the fact that in many cases the wife tends to care more for her relatives and parents than for her husband's parents and vice versa. One tends to forget that when one gets married one is creating a family bond with the family members of one's partner and obviously there are some responsibilities. However, one should care much more for one's own married life.

And parents should see to it that they do not interfere without reflection in the life of their married children. Parents should not forget that they have agreed and trusted the son or daughter in law. In fact, they have done the most appropriate thing, that is, they have helped the beginning of a union. Without the parents, there would be no husband, no wife. Their contribution to the spiritual journey of the couple has its own place.

Apart from parents, a child also can be the cause of disturbance in the couple. The child is, of course, not responsible for that. The cause lies with the immaturity of the couple. There is a sort of jealousy that comes most of the time from the husband. A new life has come and the attachment of a mother to her child is very strong as she has borne it for nine months in her womb. Obviously, she focuses much attention on it. As a child is a soul that has been invited, it should be given the best of care and attention. This, however, does not imply that the husband should be given secondary importance. Both have contributed to bring a new life. Therefore, both should be on loving terms so that they can support the child and care for its growth. Many a time both partners will be called upon to sacrifice their own time and pleasure in order to help the child to live happily and in good health.

The hope and expectation that a marriage is a perpetual honeymoon is broken when the harsh realities of life come forth. The coming of a child is one of them, especially when there is a lot to do if it is born handicapped or becomes one later on. The responsibilities that accompany a child are quite stressful. The real purpose of a married life is purely spiritual, but with the coming of a child, much energy has to be directed to it and if the couple is not sufficiently prepared, things may fall apart. Therefore I strongly recommend couples to think well before deciding to invite a soul.

If separation or divorce becomes inevitable

Life is a journey. One chooses a partner for company and also to help each other to achieve an aim. It may happen that in the course of the voyage, things do not work as expected because we cannot foresee everything. In such a case and if there is no other solution, then it is better to part with a friendly attitude. Mind you, I am not in favour of any split whatsoever but I am certainly not for suicide either, which often results from suppression of one's misery.

Normally, a break should be envisaged only when there are no children; otherwise they will have to bear the consequences. For this reason, couples should think deeply before deciding to conceive a child. Unfortunately people do not think thoroughly, or rather they refuse to reflect because it will reveal to them the truth and who really cares about the truth! It is a big problem when things start falling apart after the coming of a child. Then a great sacrifice has to be made and this demands much courage and intelligence on the part of the partners.

If a couple with children really comes to the point where divorce is inevitable, then proper arrangement for children should be worked out to ensure their well-being. The best would be to sacrifice everything for children, though this may not always be possible, especially when one is still young and wants to enjoy life. Children should be given the opportunity to share their life with both parents till a certain age or till they are able to bear the reality. This, however, is rare as it depends much on a high level of intelligence and wisdom.

The situation can become very complex and embarrassing. Say, for example, a couple decides to split but share the same roof, this may mean that each partner can have one's own private life so far as sex and social life are concerned. Will this not impact on the children? Is it possible for a couple, especially if young, to stay simply as friends just for the sake of the child? There are cases where a child is unwanted by one of the partners and the whole load of the responsibility is left upon the shoulders of the other partner. Many people's lives have become hell because they find no way out.

Much time and money is wasted unnecessarily, while enmity is bred between the two partners. They have to appear in court several times and private matters are made public. Backbiting, resentment and bickering are not uncommon. Very often, the consequence is that the children have to bear all these and they end up as emotionally or even mentally unstable individuals. They may also develop complexes. Society looks down upon such individuals. How many bother to understand that the breaking apart of the parents and their ugly behaviours are largely responsible for such situations?

Couples should be together as friends, without any attitude of possessiveness. Then if they have to part, the separation will not cause much harm to both the couple and the children. However, the best thing in the interest of the children is that the parents live together.

Another burning issue connected with divorce is the division of property. A great deal of comprehension is required here. The situation can be very complex, especially where there is '*communauté légal des biens*' and separation of wealth and so on. Such marriages are at times based on pre-thought of an eventual divorce and also on issues related to taxation and so on. The law is here to be enforced so that justice is done to both parties, but what is legal may not necessarily be correct. This may create bitterness between parties. Where the law cannot ensure a wise arrangement, wisdom, maturity, compassion and love can. However, these are not acquired from any school, parent or society. They are fruits of growth, intelligence and experience. Hence, we return to the most fundamental of all issues – a change in mentality, which itself results from mental transformation.

A divorce most of the time leads to many untowardly and complex circumstances. For example, divorced women, who have neither parents nor a house, find themselves in great difficulty. They are not always welcome by relatives. Even close ones are not ready to help as they have their own problems, or are simply inhuman. This is why, before contracting a marriage, it is good to think very deeply. The problem becomes more critical when there are children and the woman is jobless and illiterate.

Re-Marriage

People are very strange creatures. They never learn their lessons, thus they are caught in the vicious circle of suffering. Many people, after having suffered a broken marriage, remarry. They forget the problems they have gone through. It is true that at times they are compelled to do so by the force of circumstances. All these are the games of society. A divorced woman becomes a subject of harassment; she is faced with economic problems, especially if she has a few children and no qualifications. A widower or a divorced man needs a mother for his children, a person to take care of the house. Many a time, the same problems are re-encountered.

How far away people are from the aim of married life! Due to ignorance, society has created such a mess in which the poor, the ignorant and the divorced women are badly trapped. It is equally true that one should not give up easily in life. This applies to marriage too. However, is it wise to repeat the same mistake over and over again? In many cases, re-marriage leads to other types of conflicts. People should think well and know what they are expecting from married life and from the other. They should ask themselves whether their expectations are legitimate and analyse the risks of their not being fulfilled. People are fundamentally the same, thus the risk of some forms of problems cropping up is always there – no matter how many times people change partners. Hence a re-marriage should be wisely considered.

The issue of re-marriage is very complex, especially when one or both parties have children. The risk of incest and other forms of abuse always exists, thus one may find oneself in a worse situation. A re-marriage should be well considered with a frank discussion between the two parties and certain agreements should be made. My advice is that if a person is economically independent, then it is better to live without marrying again. Nevertheless, if one has no aim and nothing to focus on, then life will become boring and absurd. Spiritual people can always continue to dedicate their life to the inner adventure, which requires much time and energy.

It is sad and even stupid to contract a second marriage solely for sex, for economic support, to find a mother or a father for the children and to have support for one's old days. Most of the time it is a great disappointment, yet people do not stop and reflect deeply over it. Even if a few do, they find no way out. This is why I say that we need a great revolution. The whole system has to be changed. Our perspective of life is false; we need to have a fresh look at life. Only that can bring a positive change. Such a perspective does not come about by itself. We need to de-programme and de-condition our mind. At present, we are like a rudderless boat, carried away by the sea and we are not only helpless but also unconscious. We have compromised with that state of affairs and compromise kills our individuality.

Conclusion

The secret to a successful marriage is not miraculous and certainly not intellectual but definitely mystical. Let it be learnt and understood that marriage is a stage in the university of life and that one is free to go through it and also free to skip it. It is all a question of temperament.

If one decides to pass through it, then one should be well prepared. Here I am not talking of the kind of preparation that exists today. I mean that one should realise oneself first, know the real nature of the opposite sex, the reason why one wants to get married and what one expects from married life. One should also develop the courage to face truth, know the differences of one's partner and above all have intelligence and love. Love is deep within us and beyond the senses, feelings and personal ambitions.

Life is a pilgrimage. One should seek a partner, not an object or a slave as companion. However, one should not feel scared to take the journey of life alone. If one does not have the courage to go against established standards and norms, then one will be burying one's own nature. A lot of things have to be considered when choosing one's partner. First of all, one should not get carried away by the sex drive or sensual pull. A partner should be absolutely frank about his or her real character, weaknesses and inclinations to the other partner.

Today people divorce even though the courtship was long enough to enable them to know and understand each other. We may be born with a certain character or we may have been brought up in a way that has resulted into the development of certain traits, but the question is: are we ready to learn and change if need be? People do not change and the reason for this is that a change means losing something. And since we identify ourselves with that particular thing, for example feelings, manner, belief, conditioning and others, we feel that change means dying or losing a part of us. Our real nature is beyond change but our minds and hearts need a great cleansing. Without this transformation, I see no possibility of success in married life.

We need to grow in love and intelligence before we contract a marriage. Right now there may be only a few persons who are filled with real love and intelligence. Osho was against marriage not because he was really against it, but he maintained that people need to grow in love and intelligence first and then marry so that their children do not become neurotic like themselves. There are so many people whose evil nature is manifesting itself on the surface, yet they are marrying and having children. Try to imagine what kind of twist there will be in their lives. Do we give only our chromosomes to our offspring? Do we not pass on to them our traits too? The ultimate solution is always a complete transformation of the mind and the heart. This once again directs us to the ultimate science of meditation.

From marriage come children and with children parents are born and then a family comes into existence. Families together make a society and from society a nation is born. Therefore, for a nation to be sane, the first unit of society should be healthy. A couple forms a unit. If their union is sacred, then the offspring will be intelligent and creative. From such persons is born a powerful and loving nation.

The common concept of marriage is a major cause of divorce: no such marriage, no divorce! This may seem absurd yet it is true. The way marriages are performed leads to possessiveness, attachment and bondage. A new approach to family life should be adopted because marriages as they are performed today are a borrowed traditional system that is being followed blindly. And though it is always failing, people are helplessly and stupidly following it like sheep. It is high time to review the type of couple relationship if we wish to form a sane family because the traditional ones have failed.

It is high time that people realise that marriage nowadays has lost its true meaning and purpose and thus has been reduced to mere conformity to traditional and social norms. Should we not reflect profoundly on its implications and responsibilities and on whether we are capable to face them? It is amazing that despite the high rate of unsuccessful marriages, the young do not question the institution. Instead they blindly jump into it. Feelings and desire are strong indeed and habits die hard!

Souls merge in silence. When both the heart and the mind have reached a very high degree of inner silence, then all barriers break and there is no longer husband and wife. Then it is oneness. This is not an impossible achievement, but a tremendous and beautiful potential in each of us. This is the real meaning of marriage. Now tell me, dear reader, what does this have to do with the pomp, display and sensuous activities of the today's marriage ceremonies? The end of a married life is Ardhanareswar, as explained earlier. The conflicts that we witness in our society today are caused in great part because men and women have not yet come together on a spiritual level, they are not yet Ardhanareswar. Instead, we have been quarrelling with each other, and we still are.

"Man and woman, do not consider each other as your enemy, otherwise you will gain nothing but failure. Be ready not to conquer each other, but to merge your forces for your own good. Your marriage should be in body, mind, heart and soul, while bearing in mind your freedom."

www.ingramcontent.com/pod-product-compliance
Ingram Content Group UK Ltd.
Pitfield, Milton Keynes, MK11 3LW, UK
UKHW020140250726
13967UKWH00002B/766

9 781425 132866